THE PIE COOKBOOK

DEVELOPED BY
WILLIAMS
SONOMA
TEST KITCHEN

Photographs **Eva Kolenko**

weldon**owen**

MAKING
PERFECT
PIES

A flaky, buttery pie is a thing of beauty. Whether filled with juicy ripe peaches, sweetly spiced pumpkin, or earthy chicken and mushrooms, it's always an event—a treat that elicits smiles and exclamations of delight. Pie is perfect for a gathering of friends, a family picnic, a birthday celebration, or any occasion at all. But as wonderful as a pie can be, it can also be a bit intimidating to make.

We're here to help you master the basics. We want pie to become a mainstay in your kitchen—a joyful experience that brings the whole family together. Whether your favorite is an extravagant chocolate-and-cream fantasy or a classic apple-cinnamon pie, we've got you covered.

Pies start with a great flavorful crust. We share tips and tricks for achieving a tender crust (don't overwork it) and rolling it out easily, and we explain simple decorative elements that will set your pies apart. Along with our foolproof basic crust, there are recipes for chocolate, gingernsnap, pretzel, shortbread, cream cheese, cookie crumb, and graham cracker crusts, plus some inventive doughs flecked with herbs, and even a gluten-free dough that can be used in any recipe which calls for a basic pie dough.

The recipes for scrumptious fillings range from nearly every kind of seasonal fruit imaginable to coconut, chocolate, and lemon-buttermilk custards. We also include an array of savory main-dish pies, chock-full of meats, cheeses, vegetables, and eggs.

So pull out your rolling pin, dust your countertop with flour, and let's start baking. Trust us, it's easy as pie!

ESSENTIAL TOOLS

*To create beautiful pies, you need just a smooth work surface
for rolling out the dough and the following useful tools.*

Food processor

We recommend making pie dough in a food processor using a standard blade or a dough blade. The dough comes together quickly, and you don't risk warming up the dough with your hands. If you don't have a food processor, you can make dough by hand using a pastry blender or two table knives.

Pie dishes

A standard-sized pie dish is 9 inches (23 cm) in diameter and 1½ inches (4 cm) deep and is used for most of the pies in this cookbook. Some recipes require a deep-dish pie dish, which are 2–4 inches (5–10 cm) deep. Pie dishes are made of glass, metal, or ceramic. We love the way that glass conducts heat, plus you can see if the bottom of the crust is nicely browned. If using a metal pie dish, choose a thick, sturdy steel one.

Rolling pins

A wooden pin with a heavy cylinder that rolls independently of its two handles works well with sturdy pie dough, but there are numerous types available.

Metal or plastic dough scraper

When rolling out the dough, it's important that it doesn't stick to the work surface. A dusting of flour helps, but to easily move the dough around and to loosen it when it does stick, a scraper works wonders.

Pie weights

When partially or fully baking a pie shell before filling it (see page 13), you will need pie weights to help the crust hold its shape during baking. You can purchase ceramic pie weights (which look like small balls), or use dried beans or uncooked rice.

Cutters

A paring knife, pizza wheel, and/or kitchen shears are all helpful when trimming excess dough from a lined pie dish or cutting out strips of dough (with the help of a ruler) for a lattice top.

TIPS & TECHNIQUES

Making a great pie starts with the dough. In order to achieve a tender, flaky, and flavorful crust, it's important to not develop the gluten in the dough or you'll wind up with a flat, tough crust. What's the secret? Keep your ingredients cold and don't overwork the dough. Here are more tried-and-true tips to guarantee success every time.

Dough

- Use very cold butter, straight from the refrigerator.
- Be sure the butter is unsalted.
- Use very cold water (or other liquid, depending on the recipe). Combine ice and water in a measuring cup and then measure the water from that, avoiding the ice.
- Use a food processor to keep your warm hands off of the dough.
- Be careful not to overmix the dough; just pulse the ingredients in the processor.
- Cut the butter into cubes, then add it to the dry ingredients in the processor and pulse just until the butter is the size of peas.
- Add the ice water and pulse just until the liquid is evenly dispersed. The dough will look crumbly, but it should come together when pressed firmly. If it crumbles, add more ice water, a tablespoonful at a time, and pulse just until the dough holds together when pinched.
- Dump the dough onto a well-floured work surface and press it into a disk.
- Wrap the dough in plastic wrap.
- Chill the dough in the refrigerator for at least 30 minutes before using.
- To make the pie dough gluten-free, simply use the Gluten-Free Dough (page 91) in any recipe that calls for Basic Pie Dough.

Fruit fillings and thickeners

- Choose fresh, ripe, in-season fruit for the best flavor and texture.
- Depending on the sweetness and juiciness of the fruit, as well as your own palate, adjust the amount of sugar you add—more for unripe or less-flavorful fruit and less for very ripe, sweet fruit.
- Fruit pies need thickeners so they aren't runny. Cornstarch is our preferred thickener in this cookbook, especially for summer fruits. Potato starch or tapioca starch are also excellent options.

Egg mixture

For double-crust and lattice-topped pies, brush the top of the dough with an egg wash, a mixture of one large egg beaten with about 1 teaspoon water for a shiny, golden brown crust that helps turbinado sugar or other finishing toppings to adhere to the crust.

Cooling

Fruit pies straight out of the oven smell terrific, but they are also excessively juicy. Resist the temptation to cut into it immediately! A fruit pie needs to cool completely, for at least 4 hours, but preferably overnight, to allow the juices to gel and the pie to hold its shape when sliced. Custard pies need time in the refrigerator to set up properly and are best eaten cool. Savory pies, on the other hand, are designed to be eaten hot or warm.

ROLLING OUT PIE DOUGH

FLUTING PIE DOUGH

CRIMPING PIE DOUGH

Rolling out pie dough

Remove the chilled dough disk from the refrigerator. If the dough is too cold and firm to roll out, let it stand at room temperature for about 10 minutes (or less if it's a really warm day). Dust a flat work surface and a rolling pin with flour, then place the dough disk in the center of the work surface.

Starting from the center and rolling toward the edges in all directions, roll out the dough into a round. For a 9-inch (23-cm) pie, roll it out to about 12 inches (30 cm) in diameter and about ⅛ inch (3 mm) thick. Use firm pressure and work quickly to prevent the dough from becoming too warm. If it starts to get overly warm, carefully place it on a baking sheet and refrigerate for a few minutes.

As you roll, lift and rotate the dough several times to make sure it doesn't stick to the work surface, dusting the surface and the rolling pin with flour as needed. Flip the disk over occasionally, especially when you first start, as this helps to keep the dough smooth. If the dough does stick, carefully loosen it with a dough scraper, lightly flour the work surface, and continue to roll. Don't worry if it tears slightly; just press it back together and keep rolling.

Lining a pie dish with dough

Gently roll the dough loosely around the rolling pin and then unroll it over the pie dish, roughly centering it. Lift the edges to allow the dough to settle evenly into the bottom and sides of the dish, being careful not to stretch or tear the dough. Then trim the edges, leaving a 1-inch (2.5-cm) overhang.

Fluting or crimping pie dough

Whether you make a single-crust, double-crust, or lattice pie, you need to create a finished edge to help the crust stay in place during baking and to give your pie a professional look.

To flute, hold your index finger and thumb about 1 inch (2.5 cm) apart and press them against the outer edge of the pastry rim while pressing with your other index finger from the inside edge of the rim. Repeat all along the rim at 1-inch (2.5-cm) intervals.

To crimp, use the tines of a fork to seal the dough around the edge of the pastry rim.

Prebaking a single crust

With certain pies, you need to partially or fully bake the pie shell before filling it: when a single-crust pie has a filling that might not bake as long as the piecrust (as with custard pies), and when a pie has a cooked filling and the pie will not return to the oven.

First, roll out the dough and line and crimp the pie shell, then place it in the freezer until hard, about 30 minutes. This will help the pie shell retain its shape when prebaking. Line the inside of the frozen shell with aluminum foil and fill with pie weights (see page 8) before placing in the oven. The weights help prevent the pie from losing its shape or shrinking during baking.

For a partially baked crust, remove it from the oven when it is lightly browned on the edges and the bottom looks dry. For a fully baked crust, bake until the crust is cooked through and golden brown. Let the crust cool completely before adding the filling.

Making a classic lattice crust

A lattice-topped pie is a double-crust pie with a top woven from strips of dough and is usually used with fruit pies. First, roll out and line the pie dish with one dough round. Do not trim the overhang. Fill the pie as directed in your recipe, then roll out the second dough disk so that it is large enough to cover the entire pie, ideally with about a 1-inch (2.5-cm) overhang. Using a ruler as a guide, cut as many dough strips as you can, each 1 inch (2.5 cm) wide.

Lay half of the strips on top of the filled pie, spacing them evenly apart and leaving some space between them. Fold back every other strip halfway and lay down a strip perpendicular across the unfolded strips, then unfold the strips back into place. Fold back the alternate strips, and repeat to lay down a strip perpendicular. Repeat to place the remaining strips of dough evenly across the top, folding back the alternate strips each time. Roll together the ends of the lattice strips and the overhanging edge of the bottom crust so that they sit atop the rim of the pie dish. Flute or crimp the edge (see page 13). Brush the lattice crust with egg mixture and sprinkle with turbinado sugar, if desired.

Making a modern lattice crust (thick and thin lattice strips)

Follow the directions for creating a classic lattice crust, but cut half of the strips about 2 inches (5 cm) wide and the other half about ¾ inch (2 cm) wide. Weave the lattice together, alternating between the thick and thin strips, and finish as directed.

Making a thick lattice crust

Follow the directions for creating a classic lattice crust, but cut all of the strips about 1½ inches (4 cm) wide. Lay the strips on the pie as directed so they are nearly touching. Weave the lattice together and finish as directed.

Making braided dough strips

You can use braided dough strips as part of a lattice crust or to decorate the edges of a pie (see Gingered Peach-Blackberry Pie, page 27). Roll out a round of pie dough so that it is large enough to cover your pie. Using a ruler as a guide, cut three strips of dough, each about ¼ inch (6 mm) wide. Braid the strips together, pinching the pieces at each end to secure them. Repeat until you have three or four braided strips. Roll out another dough round and line the pie dish, add the filling, and trim the overhang evenly with the rim of the pie dish. Brush the edge of the dough with egg mixture, then lay the braided strips around the rim, pressing them into the edge of the dough. Trim as needed. If using a braid in the lattice, substitute one or two lattice strips with a braid and form the lattice pattern.

Preparing a double-crust pie

A double-crust pie is a pie shell that is filled and then topped with a second round of dough. First, roll out and line the pie dish with one dough round. Do not trim the overhang. Fill the pie as directed in your recipe (usually a fruit filling), then roll out the second dough disk so that it is large enough to cover the entire pie, ideally with about a 1-inch (2.5-cm) overhang. Trim the bottom and top crusts together so they are even. Roll the dough underneath itself so that it sits atop the rim of the pie dish, then flute or crimp the edge (see page 13). Brush the top of the dough with egg mixture and sprinkle with turbinado sugar, if desired.

FRUIT PIES

SALTED CARAMEL APPLE PIE

There is no pie that is more classic than an apple pie. Our favorite baking apples are Gala, but Granny Smith or Pink Lady apples also make a great pie. Look for baking apples with great sweet-tart flavor that hold their shape and don't turn to mush.

2 recipes Basic Pie Dough (page 90), rolled into 2 rounds

1½ cups (12 oz/375 g) granulated sugar

1 tablespoon, plus 1 teaspoon fresh lemon juice

1½ cups (375 ml) heavy cream

2 teaspoons sea salt

5 lb (2½ kg) Granny Smith apples, peeled, cored, and each apple cut into 8 slices

½ cup (3½ oz/105 g) firmly packed light brown sugar

½ teaspoon cinnamon

¼ teaspoon ground nutmeg

3 tablespoons cornstarch

1 large egg beaten with 1 teaspoon water

Turbinado sugar, for sprinkling

Flake sea salt, for sprinkling

SERVES 8–10

1   Make the pie dough. Fit 1 dough round into a 9-inch (23-cm) deep-dish pie dish and trim the edges flush with the rim. Refrigerate for 30 minutes.

2   In a large saucepan over medium heat, combine the granulated sugar, ¼ cup (60 ml) water, and the 1 teaspoon lemon juice. Cook until the mixture bubbles vigorously and turns a golden amber color, about 9 minutes. Remove from the heat and carefully add the cream, stirring until the sauce is blended. Stir in 1½ teaspoons of the salt and let cool until just warm.

3   Meanwhile, preheat the oven to 350°F (180°C).

4   In a large pot over medium heat, stir together the apples, brown sugar, cinnamon, nutmeg, and the 1 tablespoon lemon juice. Cover and cook, stirring occasionally, until the apples are just tender, 10–12 minutes. Uncover and let cool to room temperature. Stir in the cornstarch, the remaining ½ teaspoon salt, and ¾ cup (180 ml) of the sauce to the apple mixture and stir together; reserve the remaining sauce for serving.

5   Pour the filling into the crust. Place the remaining dough round over the filling, trim the edges flush with the rim, and press the top and bottom crusts together. Brush the crust with the egg mixture and sprinkle with turbinado sugar. Place the pie dish on a baking sheet.

6   Bake until the crust is golden brown and the filling is bubbling, about 1 hour, covering the top and edges with aluminum foil if they brown too quickly. Let cool on a wire rack for at least 4 hours, preferably overnight, before serving.

7   Reheat the reserved sauce over low heat until just warm. Sprinkle the pie with flake salt, slice, and serve with the sauce.

 TIP   TO SAVE TIME, USE STORE-BOUGHT CARAMEL SAUCE INSTEAD OF THE HOMEMADE VERSION HERE.

POACHED-PEAR PIE WITH ROSEMARY SHORTBREAD CRUST

Beautiful deeply red pears poached in red wine with star anise and cinnamon not only taste incredible but will make your home smell amazing. With a rosemary crust and a rich mascarpone filling, this is sure to become a modern favorite.

3 cups (750 ml)
dry red wine

¼ cup (2 oz/60 g) sugar

1 strip lemon zest, about
3 inches (7.5 cm) long

½ cup (125 ml) fresh
lemon juice

1 cinnamon stick

1 star anise pod

1 fresh rosemary sprig

4 firm but ripe pears (about
2 lb/1 kg total weight),
peeled, halved, and cored

1 recipe Rosemary
Shortbread Crust (page
99), baked and cooled

1 cup (8 oz/250 g)
mascarpone cheese

⅓ cup (80 ml) heavy cream

1 teaspoon pure
vanilla extract

¼ cup (2 oz/60 g) sugar

SERVES 8–10

1   In a large saucepan over high heat, combine the wine, sugar, lemon zest and juice, cinnamon stick, and star anise and bring to a boil. Reduce the heat to medium-low, add the rosemary sprig, and simmer for about 5 minutes. Add the pears, making sure they are mostly submerged. Simmer, turning them every 5 minutes, until just fork-tender but still firm, 15–20 minutes. Let cool to room temperature in the liquid. Refrigerate in the liquid, cut side down, for at least 2 hours or up to overnight.

2   Make the rosemary shortbread crust.

3   In the bowl of a stand mixer fitted with the whisk attachment, combine the mascarpone cheese, cream, and vanilla. On low speed, slowly add the sugar. Raise the speed to medium-high and beat until stiff peaks form, about 30 seconds. Pipe or spoon the filling over the crust.

4   Using a slotted spoon, gently remove the pears from the liquid and cut each half into slices ¼ inch (6 mm) thick, keeping the slices attached at the stem end and fanning them slightly. Arrange the pears over the filling. Remove and discard the cinnamon stick, star anise, and rosemary sprig. Transfer the liquid to a small saucepan and simmer over medium-high heat until thickened, about 10 minutes. Let cool to room temperature. Drizzle over the pie. Refrigerate for at least 1 hour or up to overnight before serving.

 TIP   **FOR DEEPER COLOR AND FLAVOR, POACH THE PEARS THE DAY BEFORE AND REFRIGERATE OVERNIGHT IN THEIR POACHING LIQUID. USE A DRY RED WINE, SUCH AS A CABERNET SAUVIGNON OR MERLOT.**

STRAWBERRY-RHUBARB CRUMBLE PIE

Sweet springtime fruits shine in this delicious pie topped with crunchy oat-based streusel. Whether you use a strawberry-rhubarb combination, all berries, or all rhubarb, you are certain to bring smiles to everyone's faces.

1 recipe Basic Pie Dough (page 90), rolled into 1 round

1 recipe Oat Crumble Topping (page 98)

1 cup (8 oz/250 g) sugar

⅓ cup (1½ oz/45 g) cornstarch

1 teaspoon kosher salt

3 pints (1½ lb/750 g) strawberries, stemmed, cored, and thickly sliced

1½ lb (750 g) rhubarb, trimmed and cut into ¾-inch (2-cm) pieces

1 teaspoon grated orange zest

2 teaspoons fresh orange juice

Vanilla ice cream, for serving

SERVES 8–10

1   Make the pie dough. Fit the dough round into a 9-inch (23-cm) pie dish. Trim the overhang to ½ inch (12 mm), fold the edge under itself, and decoratively flute or crimp. Pierce the bottom of the crust all over with a fork and freeze for 30 minutes.

2   Make the crumble topping.

3   Preheat the oven to 375°F (190°C).

4   In a large bowl, whisk together the sugar, cornstarch, and salt. Add the strawberries and rhubarb and stir to combine. Let stand for 20 minutes, then drain off the excess liquid. Stir in the orange zest and juice. Pour the filling into the crust. Sprinkle with the crumble topping and place the pie dish on a baking sheet.

5   Bake until the crust is golden brown and the filling is bubbling, 45–55 minutes, covering the top and edges with aluminum foil if they brown too quickly. Let cool on a wire rack for at least 4 hours, preferably overnight, before serving. Serve with vanilla ice cream.

 TIP IF YOU CAN'T FIND RHUBARB, MAKE AN ALL-STRAWBERRY PIE OR SUBSTITUTE ANOTHER FRESH BERRY TO TOTAL 3 LB (1.5 KG) OF FRUIT.

GINGERED PEACH-BLACKBERRY PIE

For braided edges, add and trim the lattice (see page 14), then roll out a dough square that is a little larger than the pan and cut it into 12 thin strips. Braid 3 strips for each side, egg wash the edges, press the braids into place, and trim any excess.

2 recipes Basic Pie Dough
(page 90)

All-purpose flour,
for dusting

8 cups (3 lb/1.5 kg) peeled
fresh or thawed frozen
peach slices (from about
7–8 fresh peaches)

2 pints (1 lb/500 g) fresh or
thawed frozen blackberries

¾ cup (6 oz/185 g) firmly
packed light brown sugar

1 tablespoon fresh
lemon juice

¼ cup (1 oz/30 g)
cornstarch

1½ teaspoons minced
peeled fresh ginger

Pinch of kosher salt

1 large egg beaten with
1 teaspoon water

Turbinado sugar,
for sprinkling

SERVES 8–10

1 Make the pie dough. Preheat the oven to 350°F (180°C).

2 On a lightly floured work surface, roll out 1 dough disk into a 12½-inch (31.5-cm) square. Roll the dough around the rolling pin and unroll it into an 8-inch (20-cm) square deep baking dish. Gently press the dough into the bottom and sides of the dish. Trim the edges flush with the trim. Refrigerate for 30 minutes.

3 In a large bowl, toss together the peaches and blackberries. Add the brown sugar, lemon juice, cornstarch, ginger, and salt and toss until well combined. Pour the filling into the crust.

4 Transfer the remaining dough round to a work surface and cut into lattice strips. Arrange the dough strips in a lattice form (see page 14). Brush the crust with the egg mixture and sprinkle with turbinado sugar. Place the pie dish on a baking sheet.

5 Bake until the crust is golden brown and the filling is bubbling, 1–1¼ hours, covering the top and edges with aluminum foil if they brown too quickly. Let cool on a wire rack for at least 4 hours, preferably overnight, before serving.

 TIP TO MAKE THIS RECIPE IN A 9-INCH (23-CM) ROUND PIE DISH, HALVE THE FILLING INGREDIENTS.

CRANBERRY PIE

This jewel-toned lattice-topped pie is a great way to finish a hearty feast. For the holidays, instead of a lattice-topped pie, use a holiday-themed cookie cutter to cut out pieces of rolled-out pie dough and then layer them over the top in a pretty pattern.

2 recipes Basic Pie Dough (page 90), rolled into 2 rounds

9 cups (2¼ lb/1.1 kg) fresh or thawed frozen cranberries

2¼ cups (1 lb/500 g) firmly packed light brown sugar

¼ cup (1 oz/30 g) plus 1 tablespoon cornstarch

1½ tablespoons grated orange zest

½ cup (125 ml) fresh orange juice

1 teaspoon cinnamon

¼ teaspoon ground nutmeg

¼ teaspoon ground cloves

1 teaspoon pure vanilla extract

1 large egg beaten with 1 teaspoon water

Turbinado sugar, for sprinkling

SERVES 10

1   Make the pie dough. Fit 1 dough round into a 9-inch (23-cm) deep-dish pie dish and trim the edges flush with the rim. Refrigerate for 30 minutes.

2   Meanwhile, preheat the oven to 350°F (180°C).

3   In a large pot pan over medium heat, combine the cranberries, brown sugar, cornstarch, orange zest and juice, cinnamon, nutmeg, and cloves. Cook, stirring occasionally, until the cranberries soften and release their juice, 8–10 minutes. Stir in the vanilla and let cool to room temperature.

4   Pour the filling into the crust. Using the remaining dough round, create a modern lattice pattern (see page 14). Brush the crust with the egg mixture and sprinkle with turbinado sugar. Place the pie dish on a baking sheet.

5   Bake until the crust is golden brown and the filling is bubbling, about 1 hour, covering the top and edges with aluminum foil if they brown too quickly. Let cool on a wire rack for at least 4 hours, preferably overnight, before serving.

 TIP THIS RECIPE CALLS FOR A DEEP-DISH PIE DISH. IF USING A REGULAR-SIZED PIE DISH, HALVE THE FILLING INGREDIENTS.

PEACH PIE

A bountiful, juicy peach pie is the epitome of summertime. This sunny dessert is best made when peaches are at their ripe, fragrant best late in the season. We love the simplicity of this pie with just a scoop of vanilla ice cream.

2 recipes Basic Pie Dough (page 90), rolled into 2 rounds

2 lb (1 kg) peaches, peeled, pitted, and sliced

1 tablespoon fresh lemon juice

⅓ cup (3 oz/90 g) granulated sugar

2 tablespoons cornstarch

¼ teaspoon kosher salt

Pinch of cinnamon

1 large egg beaten with 1 teaspoon water

Turbinado sugar, for sprinkling

SERVES 8-10

1   Make the pie dough. Fit 1 dough round into a 9-inch (23-cm) deep-dish pie dish and trim the edges flush with the rim. Refrigerate the pie shell and the remaining dough round for 30 minutes.

2   Meanwhile, preheat the oven to 350°F (180°C).

3   In a large bowl, toss together the peaches and lemon juice. In a small bowl, stir together the granulated sugar, cornstarch, salt, and cinnamon. Add to the peaches and toss to combine. Pour the filling into the crust.

4   Transfer the remaining dough round to a work surface and cut into lattice strips. Arrange the dough strips in a tight lattice form (see page 14). Brush the crust with the egg mixture and sprinkle with turbinado sugar. Place the pie dish on a baking sheet.

5   Bake until the crust is golden brown and the filling is bubbling, 45–50 minutes, covering the top and edges with aluminum foil if they brown too quickly. Let cool on a wire rack for at least 4 hours, preferably overnight, before serving.

 TIP   IN PLACE OF PEACHES, TRY FRESH NECTARINES. FROZEN PEACHES ALSO WORK WELL; BE SURE TO THAW THEM AND DRAIN OFF THE LIQUID.

BLUEBERRY-CARDAMOM PIE

Cardamom adds a warm, exotic note to this otherwise classic pie. Be sure to use the full amount of thickener, as blueberries can be very juicy, especially when they are fresh and sweet in early summer.

2 recipes Basic Pie Dough (page 90)

4 pints (2 lb/1 kg) fresh or thawed frozen blueberries

1¼ cups (10 oz/315 g) granulated sugar

1 teaspoon grated lemon zest

2 tablespoons fresh lemon juice

½ teaspoon ground cardamom

Pinch of kosher salt

¼ cup (1 oz/30 g) cornstarch

2 tablespoons unsalted butter, diced

1 large egg beaten with 1 teaspoon water

Turbinado sugar, for sprinkling

SERVES 8-10

1 Make the pie dough. Roll 1 dough into a round and fit into a 9-inch (23-cm) deep-dish pie dish and trim the overhang to ½ inch (12 mm), fold the edge under itself, and decoratively flute. Refrigerate the pie shell and the remaining dough for 30 minutes.

2 Meanwhile, preheat the oven to 350°F (180°C).

3 In a large saucepan over medium heat, combine the blueberries, granulated sugar, lemon zest and juice, cardamom, and salt. Cook, stirring occasionally, until some of the berries begin to burst and the liquid reduces slightly, 5-7 minutes. Remove from the heat and fold in the cornstarch. Let cool to room temperature.

4 Transfer the remaining dough to a work surface and roll out into a long rectangle, about 6-by-18-inches (15-by-45-cm). Cut the rectangle lengthwise into six 1-inch (2.5-cm) wide strips. Remove the pie shell from the refrigerator, pour in the filling, and dot with the butter. Carefully twist 1 strip of dough. Starting at the center of the pie, gently lay the twisted strip of dough in a circular pattern. Pinch the end of a second strip to the first to seal, then twist and coil the second strip around the first. Continue to add the remaining dough strips, circling them over the pie filling. Brush the crust with the egg mixture and sprinkle with turbinado sugar. Place the pie dish on a baking sheet.

5 Bake until the crust is golden brown and the filling is bubbling, 50-55 minutes, covering the top and edges with aluminum foil if they brown too quickly. Let cool on a wire rack for at least 4 hours, preferably overnight, before serving.

 TIP TRY OTHER TYPES OF BERRIES, SUCH AS BLACKBERRIES OR STRAWBERRIES OR A COMBINATION.

APPLE HAND PIES

Perfect for a picnic, these adorable little pies have the added surprise of pistachios, which you can leave out if you like, but we don't recommend it. You can make these in all different shapes: rounds as instructed, squares, or folded over into triangles or half circles.

2 recipes Basic Pie Dough (page 90), rolled into 2 rounds

¼ cup (2 oz/60 g) granulated sugar

2 lb (1 kg) Pink Lady or Fuji apples, peeled, cored, and cut into ⅛-inch (3-mm) slices

1 teaspoon cinnamon

¼ teaspoon ground cardamom

¼ teaspoon kosher salt

½ cup (2 oz/60 g) unsalted pistachios, toasted and chopped

Zest and juice of 1 lemon

1 large egg beaten with 1 teaspoon water

Turbinado sugar, for sprinkling

Vanilla ice cream, for serving

MAKES 10 HAND PIES

1   Make the pie dough. Using a 4-inch (10-cm) round cutter, cut out 20 rounds, gathering the scraps of dough and rerolling as needed. Cover with plastic wrap and refrigerate until ready to use. Let stand at room temperature for about 10 minutes before assembling the pies.

2   In a large sauté pan over medium heat, combine the granulated sugar and ¾ cup (180 ml) water and cook, stirring, until the sugar is dissolved. Add the apples, cinnamon, cardamom, and salt. Cook, stirring occasionally, until the apples are just tender and the liquid is slightly thickened, 6–8 minutes. Transfer to a bowl and stir in the pistachios and lemon zest and juice. Let cool to room temperature.

3   Meanwhile, preheat the oven to 400°F (200°C). Line a baking sheet with parchment paper.

4   Space half of the dough rounds on the prepared baking sheet, at least 1 inch (2.5 cm) apart. Brush them with some of the egg mixture, then place about ¼ cup (1 oz/30 g) of the apple filling in the center of each. Top each with a remaining dough round. Press top and bottom edges together, then crimp with a fork. Brush the tops with the egg mixture and cut small steam vents. Sprinkle with turbinado sugar.

5   Bake until the crust is golden brown, 18–22 minutes. Let cool for 5 minutes. Serve warm or at room temperature with a scoop of vanilla ice cream.

 TIP   MINI TART PANS ALSO WORK GREAT IN THIS RECIPE. LINE EACH WELL WITH A PIE DOUGH ROUND, THEN FILL, TOP WITH ANOTHER ROUND, AND BAKE AS DIRECTED.

CHERRY SLAB PIE

If you are feeding a crowd, there's nothing better than a slab pie, which can be made in a deep rimmed baking sheet. Because the pie doesn't have a base, it's easy to serve up big scoops. Try this with other summer fruits at your next barbecue.

2 recipes Basic Pie Dough (page 90), rolled into 2 rounds

14 cups pitted fresh or thawed frozen cherries (about 4½ lb/2.25 kg)

¾–1 cup (6–8 oz/185–245 g) granulated sugar (depending on the tartness of the cherries)

3 tablespoons cornstarch

1½ tablespoons almond meal

2 teaspoons grated lemon zest

1½ teaspoons almond extract

Pinch of kosher salt

1 large egg beaten with 1 teaspoon water

Turbinado sugar, for sprinkling

SERVES 10–12

1   Make the pie dough. Preheat the oven to 350°F (180°C).

2   In a large bowl, toss together the cherries, ¾ cup (6 oz/185 g) of the granulated sugar, the cornstarch, almond meal, lemon zest, almond extract, and salt. Taste and add up to ¼ cup (2 oz/60 g) more sugar, if desired. Transfer the filling to a rimmed half sheet pan and spread evenly.

3   Using a 3-inch (7.5-cm) round cutter, cut out enough rounds to cover the pie, gathering the scraps of dough and rerolling as needed. Place the rounds over the pie filling, overlapping slightly. Brush the crust with the egg mixture and sprinkle with turbinado sugar.

4   Bake until the crust is golden brown and the filling is bubbling, about 45 minutes, covering the top with aluminum foil if it browns too quickly. Let cool on a wire rack for at least 4 hours, preferably overnight, before serving.

 TOP YOUR SLAB PIE WITH WHATEVER CUTOUT SHAPES YOU LIKE. STARS WOULD LOOK FESTIVE FOR THE FOURTH OF JULY, WHILE HEARTS WOULD BE PERFECT FOR VALENTINE'S DAY.

CHOCOLATE CHECKERBOARD RASPBERRY PIE

This lattice pie uses two kinds of pie dough, chocolate and plain, for a gorgeous effect! The woven lattice hides a sweet filling of fresh raspberries spiked with Chambord. This is a great pie for your next party.

2 recipes Chocolate Pie Dough (page 93), rolled into 2 rounds

1 recipe Basic Pie Dough (page 90), rolled into 1 round

5 pints (2½ lb/1.25 kg) fresh or thawed frozen raspberries

¼ cup (1 oz/30 g) cornstarch

1 cup (8 oz/250 g) granulated sugar

2 tablespoons Chambord raspberry liqueur

Zest of 1 lemon

Pinch of kosher salt

1 large egg beaten with 1 teaspoon water

Turbinado sugar, for sprinkling

SERVES 6–8

1   Make both pie doughs. Fit the dough round into a 9-inch (23-cm) pie dish. Trim the overhang to ½ inch (12 mm), fold the edge under itself, and decoratively crimp. Refrigerate the pie shell and the remaining 2 dough rounds for 30 minutes.

2   Meanwhile, preheat the oven to 350°F (180°C).

3   Transfer the remaining chocolate dough round to a work surface and cut out 2-inch (5-cm) lattice strips. Repeat with the basic pie dough round. Refrigerate until ready to use.

4   In a large bowl, stir together the raspberries, cornstarch, granulated sugar, liqueur, lemon zest, and salt. Pour the filling into the crust.

5   Create a checkerboard lattice on top by laying all of the chocolate strips close together with a small gap between them on top of the filling. Weave the basic pie dough strips in a classic lattice pattern with the chocolate strips (see page 14). Trim off any excess dough. Brush the crust with the egg mixture and sprinkle with turbinado sugar. Place the pie dish on a baking sheet.

6   Bake until the crust is golden brown and the filling is bubbling, about 1 hour, covering the top and edges with aluminum foil if they brown too quickly. Let cool on a wire rack for at least 4 hours, preferably overnight, before serving.

 TIP   INSTEAD OF CHOCOLATE AND PLAIN, YOU CAN USE JUST ONE TYPE OF DOUGH. THE PIE WON'T HAVE A CHECKERBOARD EFFECT BUT WILL STILL TASTE GREAT.

SPECIAL PIES

TOASTED-COCONUT CREAM PIE

Seek out good quality shredded and flaked coconut for this fragrant and creamy pie, and be sure to choose unsweetened. Toast the flaked coconut by spreading it on a baking sheet and toasting in a 325°F (165°C) oven, stirring once or twice, for about 5 minutes.

1 recipe vanilla cookie Wafer Cookie Crust (page 90), baked and cooled

1½ cups (375 ml) whole milk

1½ cups (375 ml) coconut milk

3 large eggs plus 2 large egg yolks

¾ cup (6 oz/185 g) sugar

¼ cup (1½ oz/45 g) all-purpose flour

¼ teaspoon kosher salt

1½ teaspoons pure vanilla extract

1 cup (4 oz/125 g) shredded dried unsweetened coconut (optional)

1 recipe Whipped Cream Topping (page 96)

½ cup (1½ oz/45 g) toasted flaked unsweetened coconut

SERVES 8–10

1 Make the wafer cookie crust.

2 In a saucepan over medium heat, combine the milk and coconut milk and warm until it just begins to simmer.

3 In a large bowl, whisk together the eggs, egg yolks, sugar, flour, and salt until smooth. Add the hot milk mixture, ¼ cup (60 ml) at a time, to the egg mixture, whisking constantly, then pour the mixture back into the pan. Cook, stirring constantly over medium-high heat until the mixture boils. Reduce the heat to medium and stir constantly until the mixture is thick enough to coat the spoon, 6–8 minutes.

4 Pour the mixture through a fine-mesh sieve into a large bowl. Stir in the vanilla and shredded coconut (if using). Let cool to room temperature. Pour the filling into the crust.

5 Make the topping. Pipe or spoon the whipped cream over the pie and garnish with the flaked coconut. Refrigerate for at least 2 hours or up to overnight before serving.

 TIP FOR MORE COCONUT FLAVOR, STIR SHREDDED COCONUT INTO THE PIE FILLING. IF YOU PREFER A SILKY SMOOTH TEXTURE, LEAVE IT OUT.

DULCE DE LECHE ICE CREAM PIE

The great thing about this modern ice cream pie, besides its creamy decadence, is that it can be made up to a week ahead! Which means you can make it anytime and serve it at a moment's notice.

1 recipe vanilla cookie Wafer Cookie Crust (page 90), baked and cooled

1 cup (7 oz/220 g) firmly packed light brown sugar

½ cup (125 ml) half-and-half

4 tablespoons (2 oz/60 g) unsalted butter

1 teaspoon kosher salt

1 tablespoon pure vanilla extract

2 pints (1¾ lb/880 g) dulce de leche ice cream, softened

1⅔ cups (6½ oz/ 200 g) pecans, toasted and chopped

SERVES 8–10

1   Make the wafer cookie crust.

2   In a small saucepan over medium-low heat, combine the brown sugar, half-and-half, butter, and salt. Cook, whisking gently, until the sauce thickens, 5–7 minutes. Stir in the vanilla and cook for 1 minute longer. Transfer the caramel sauce to a small bowl and let cool to room temperature.

3   Spread 1 pint (14 oz/440 g) of the ice cream evenly over the crust. Freeze until almost firm, about 1 hour. Reserve ¼ cup (60 ml) of the caramel sauce for drizzling and spread the rest evenly over the ice cream. Layer the pecans on top, reserving ¼ cup (1 oz/30 g) of the pecans for garnish, if desired. Freeze until the caramel hardens, about 20 minutes. Spread the remaining 1 pint (14 oz/440 g) ice cream evenly over the caramel-pecan layer. Freeze until firm, about 1 hour.

4   Drizzle the reserved caramel sauce over the pie. Sprinkle the reserved pecans, if using, around the edges. Freeze until ready to serve, up to 1 week.

 TIP   **TO SOFTEN THE ICE CREAM, PLACE IT IN THE REFRIGERATOR FOR 1–2 HOURS BEFORE USING.**

PEANUT BUTTER PIE WITH PRETZEL CRUST

The beloved combination of peanut butter and chocolate are updated with a lightly salty pretzel crust. Be sure to use creamy peanut butter (or another favorite creamy nut butter) to retain the smooth texture of the pie.

1 recipe Pretzel Crust (page 91), baked and cooled

1½ cups (375 ml) heavy cream

½ lb (250 g) cream cheese, at room temperature

½ cup (2 oz/60 g) confectioners' sugar

¼ teaspoon kosher salt

1 teaspoon pure vanilla extract

1¼ cups (12½ oz/390 g) creamy peanut butter

1 recipe Whipped Cream Topping (page 96)

Melted chocolate and chopped peanut butter cups, for garnish

SERVES 8–10

1   Make the pretzel crust.

2   In the bowl of a stand mixer fitted with the whisk attachment, beat the cream on medium speed until soft peaks form, 4–5 minutes. Transfer to a bowl.

3   In the same mixer bowl using the paddle attachment, beat the cream cheese on medium speed until smooth and pliable, about 3 minutes. Add the confectioners' sugar, salt, and vanilla and beat until well combined, 1–2 minutes. Add the peanut butter and beat until smooth, 1–2 minutes.

4   Using a rubber spatula, fold the whipped cream into the peanut butter mixture until incorporated, 2–3 minutes; be careful not to overmix.

5   Pour the filling into the crust. Refrigerate for at least 2 hours or up to overnight before serving. Top with whipped cream and garnish with melted chocolate and chopped peanut butter cups.

 TIP   OTHER TYPES OF NUT BUTTERS, SUCH AS ALMOND OR CASHEW, WOULD ALSO BE DELICIOUS.

MAPLE-PECAN PIE WITH SHORTBREAD CRUST

For many, it just isn't autumn without a toasty pecan pie. The dark sweetness of maple brings out the pecan flavor and a toothsome shortbread crust is a nice contrast to the texture of this striking pie.

1 recipe Shortbread Crust
(page 98), baked
and cooled

1½ cups (16½ oz/515 g)
pure maple syrup

3 large eggs, lightly beaten

¼ cup (2 oz/60 g)
granulated sugar

¼ cup (2 oz/60 g) firmly
packed dark brown sugar

¼ teaspoon kosher salt

4 tablespoons (2 oz/60 g)
unsalted butter, melted
and cooled

1 teaspoon pure
vanilla extract

3 tablespoons
all-purpose flour

2 tablespoons heavy cream

2 cups (8 oz/250 g) pecans,
toasted and chopped

SERVES 8–10

1 Make the shortbread crust.

2 Preheat the oven to 350°F (180°C).

3 In a saucepan over medium-high heat, bring the maple syrup to a boil and boil until reduced to 1 cup (11 oz/345 g), 8–10 minutes. Let cool to room temperature.

4 In a large bowl, stir together the eggs, granulated sugar, brown sugar, reduced maple syrup, salt, melted butter, and vanilla until smooth and blended. Stir in the flour and cream and then the pecans. Pour the filling into the crust.

5 Bake until the center is slightly puffed and firm to the touch, 30–40 minutes, covering the edges with aluminum foil if they brown too quickly. Let cool on a wire rack until just slightly warm, about 45 minutes, before serving.

 TIP FOR A PRETTY VISUAL EFFECT, KEEP THE PECANS WHOLE AND ARRANGE ON TOP OF THE UNBAKED PIE INSTEAD OF STIRRING THEM INTO THE FILLING.

S'MORES PIE

With a crunchy graham cracker crust, a rich deeply chocolate filling, and clouds of vanilla-scented meringue, this decadent pie is not for the faint of heart. It will elicit oohs and ahs from all of your guests, young and old alike.

1 recipe Graham Cracker Crust (page 93), baked and cooled

2 cups (500 ml) whole milk

6 large eggs, separated

1¾ cups (14 oz/435 g) sugar

Pinch of kosher salt

3 tablespoons all-purpose flour

2 tablespoons unsweetened cocoa powder

6 oz (185 g) semisweet chocolate, finely chopped

2 oz (60 g) unsweetened chocolate, finely chopped

2 teaspoons pure vanilla extract

SERVES 8–10

1 Make the graham cracker crust.

2 In a saucepan over medium heat, warm the milk until it just begins to simmer. Remove from the heat.

3 In a bowl, whisk together the egg yolks, ¾ cup (6 oz/185 g) of the sugar, and the salt until smooth. Sift the flour and cocoa powder over the egg mixture and whisk until smooth. Add the hot milk, ¼ cup (60 ml) at a time, to the egg mixture, whisking constantly, then pour the mixture back into the pan. Stir constantly over medium heat until the mixture thickens and comes to a boil, about 4 minutes. Reduce the heat to low and stir constantly until the mixture coats the back of the spoon, about 1 minute longer.

4 Pour the mixture through a fine-mesh sieve into a large bowl. Add both chocolates and stir until melted, then stir in 1 teaspoon of the vanilla. Pour the filling into the crust. Refrigerate, uncovered, until chilled, about 2 hours.

5 In the bowl of a stand mixer, combine the egg whites and the remaining 1 cup (8 oz/250 g) sugar. Set the bowl over but not touching simmering water in a saucepan. Whisk until the sugar is dissolved and the mixture is hot to the touch, about 2 minutes. Place the bowl on the mixer fitted with the whisk attachment and add the remaining 1 teaspoon vanilla. Beat on high speed until the meringue cools to room temperature and stiff peaks form, 5–6 minutes.

6 Mound the meringue on top of the pie and lightly brown with a kitchen torch. Serve right away or refrigerate for at least 2 hours or up to overnight.

 TIP IF YOU DON'T HAVE A KITCHEN TORCH, BROWN THE MERINGUE UNDER THE BROILER FOR 5 MINUTES.

KEY LIME PIE WITH PRETZEL CRUST

Similar to a graham cracker crust, this salty-sweet pretzel shell pairs beautifully with the zesty, fragrant key lime filling. Look for bottled key lime juice, or, if you are lucky enough to find them, use fresh key limes.

1 recipe Pretzel Crust
(page 91), baked
and cooled

8 large egg yolks

2 cans (14 fl oz/
430 ml each) sweetened
condensed milk

4 teaspoons grated
lime zest

1 cup (250 ml)
Key lime juice

1 recipe Whipped Cream
Topping (page 96)

Grated lime zest, for
garnish (optional)

Turbinado sugar, for
sprinkling (optional)

SERVES 8–10

1 Make the pretzel crust. Preheat the oven to 350°F (180°C).

2 In a large bowl, whisk together the egg yolks until well blended. Add the condensed milk and lime zest and juice and whisk to combine. Pour the filling into the crust. Place the pie dish on a baking sheet.

3 Bake until the edges of the pie are set but the center still jiggles slightly, 18–22 minutes. Let cool completely on a wire rack. Refrigerate for at least 2 hours or up to overnight before serving.

4 Make the topping. Pipe or spoon the whipped cream over the cooled pie. Garnish with lime zest and sprinkle with turbinado sugar, if using.

 TIP POUR IN THE FILLING UNTIL IT JUST REACHES THE TOP OF THE PRETZEL CRUST; YOU MAY HAVE SOME LEFT OVER DEPENDING ON THE SIZE OF YOUR PIE DISH.

PUMPKIN CHAI MINI PIES

Pumpkin pie doesn't have to be only for the Thanksgiving table. Update this classic for your next autumn or winter dinner party by making sweet little individual pies with the warm, fragrant flavors of chai: cinnamon, ginger, cardamom, and cloves.

2 recipes Basic Pie Dough (page 90), rolled into 2 rounds

Nonstick cooking spray

1 can (15 oz/470 g) pumpkin puree

1 cup (7 oz/220 g) firmly packed light brown sugar

1 tablespoon cornstarch

¾ teaspoon cinnamon

¾ teaspoon ground ginger

½ teaspoon ground cardamom

½ teaspoon ground cloves

½ teaspoon kosher salt

3 large eggs, lightly beaten

1 cup (250 ml) heavy cream

1¼ teaspoons pure vanilla extract

1 recipe Whipped Cream Topping (page 96), for serving

MAKES 24 MINI PIES

1   Make the pie dough. Lightly coat 24 standard muffin cups with nonstick cooking spray. Using a 4-inch (10-cm) round cutter, cut out 24 rounds and fit them into the prepared muffin cups, gathering the scraps of dough and rerolling as needed. Trim the edges, if necessary, leaving a ¼-inch (6-mm) overhang. Freeze for 30 minutes.

2   Meanwhile, preheat the oven to 350°F (180°C).

3   Bake the crusts until dry to the touch and lightly browned, about 20 minutes. Let cool completely on wire racks. Keep the oven set.

4   In a large bowl, whisk together the pumpkin puree and brown sugar. Add the cornstarch, cinnamon, ginger, cardamom, cloves, and salt and whisk until smooth. Add the eggs and whisk until combined. Add the cream and vanilla and whisk until smooth. Divide the filling among the crusts.

5   Bake until the filling is set, 30–35 minutes, covering the edges with aluminum foil if they brown too quickly. Let cool completely on wire racks before serving. Serve each mini pie with a dollop of whipped cream.

 TIP   REPLACE THE CARDAMOM WITH ¼ TEASPOON GROUND NUTMEG FOR A MORE TRADITIONAL PUMPKIN PIE FLAVOR PROFILE.

BUTTERSCOTCH-BOURBON PIE

Plenty of dark brown sugar, brown butter, and bourbon give this butterscotch pie deep flavor. To cut the density, we like to serve it with lightly whipped cream. Be sure to choose a sweet bourbon that you'd enjoy serving alongside.

1 recipe Basic Pie Dough (page 90), rolled into 1 round

1½ cups (375 ml) whole milk

1½ cups (375 ml) heavy cream

1 vanilla bean, split and seeds scraped, seeds and pod reserved

4 tablespoons (2 oz/60 g) unsalted butter

¾ cup (6 oz/185 g) firmly packed dark brown sugar

9 large egg yolks

3 tablespoons cornstarch

1 teaspoon kosher salt

2 tablespoons bourbon

1 teaspoon fresh lemon juice

1 recipe Whipped Cream Topping (page 96), for serving

SERVES 8–10

1   Make the pie dough. Fit the dough round into a 9-inch (23-cm) pie dish. Trim the overhang to ½ inch (12 mm), fold the edge under itself, and decoratively flute or crimp. Pierce the bottom of the crust all over with a fork and freeze for 30 minutes.

2   Meanwhile, preheat the oven to 350°F (180°C). Line the crust with aluminum foil and fill with pie weights. Bake until lightly browned, about 15 minutes. Remove the foil and weights and cook completely, 10–15 minutes longer. Set on a wire rack to cool completely. Keep the oven set.

3   In a small saucepan over medium heat, combine the milk, cream, and vanilla bean seeds and pod and bring to a gentle simmer. Remove from the heat and let stand for 5 minutes. Discard the vanilla pod.

4   In a large saucepan over medium heat, melt the butter. Reduce the heat to low and cook until the milk solids are golden with a nutty fragrance, but not burned, about 6 minutes. Stir in half of the brown sugar and the milk mixture. Remove from the heat.

5   In a large bowl, whisk together the egg yolks, cornstarch, salt, and the remaining brown sugar until well blended. Add the hot milk, ¼ cup (60 ml) at a time, to the egg mixture, whisking constantly, then pour the mixture back into the pan. Stir constantly over medium-high heat until the mixture boils. Reduce the heat to medium and stir constantly until the mixture is thick enough to coat the spoon, 6–8 minutes. Pour the mixture through a fine-mesh sieve into a large bowl. Stir in the bourbon and lemon juice. Pour the filling into the crust.

6   Bake until the edges are set but the center jiggles slightly, 25–35 minutes, covering the edges with aluminum foil if they brown too quickly. Let cool completely on a wire rack. Serve at room temperature or chilled for at least 2 hours or up to overnight. Top with whipped cream and serve.

 NO VANILLA BEAN? NO PROBLEM! USE 1 TEASPOON PURE VANILLA EXTRACT INSTEAD, IN THE SAME WAY YOU USE THE VANILLA BEAN.

SALTY HONEY PIE

If you've never had or heard of salty honey pie, you are in for a treat! This custard-filled pie is similar to a chess pie or buttermilk pie, but with plenty of honey-toned flavor. For contrast, we sprinkle the top with flake sea salt.

1 recipe Basic Pie Dough (page 90), rolled into 1 round

½ cup (4 oz/125 g) unsalted butter, melted and cooled

¾ cup (3½ oz/105 g) firmly packed light brown sugar

2 tablespoons cornstarch

Pinch of kosher salt

1 teaspoon pure vanilla extract

¾ cup (9 oz/280 g) honey

3 large eggs, lightly beaten

½ cup (125 ml) heavy cream

2 teaspoons fresh lemon juice

Flake sea salt, for sprinkling

SERVES 8–10

1 Make the pie dough. Fit the dough round into a 9-inch (23-cm) deep-dish pie dish. Trim the overhang to ½ inch (12 mm), fold the edge under itself, and decoratively flute or crimp. Freeze for 30 minutes.

2 Meanwhile, preheat the oven to 350°F (180°C).

3 Line the crust with aluminum foil and fill with pie weights. Bake until lightly browned and dry to the touch, about 20 minutes. Remove the foil and weights and set on a wire rack to cool completely. Keep the oven set.

4 In a large bowl, stir together the melted butter, brown sugar, cornstarch, salt, vanilla, honey, eggs, cream, and lemon juice. Pour the filling into the crust.

5 Bake until puffed and golden brown, 45–50 minutes, covering the edges with aluminum foil if they brown too quickly. Let cool completely on a wire rack before serving. Sprinkle with flake sea salt and serve.

 TIP CHOOSE A HONEY THAT IS FLAVORFUL BUT NOT OVERPOWERING, SUCH AS WILDFLOWER OR CLOVER.

LEMON MERINGUE PIE WITH GINGERSNAP CRUST

Nothing says showstopper like a tangy-sweet lemon meringue pie piled high with billowy, light-as-a-feather meringue. For more height and drama, instead of piping the meringue, mound it on top of the pie, and then broil until lightly toasted.

1 recipe Gingersnap Crust (page 96), baked and cooled

5 large eggs plus 7 large egg yolks (save 5 egg whites for the meringue topping)

1½ cups (12 oz/375 g) sugar

⅓ cup (1½ oz/45 g) cornstarch

1½ cups (375 ml) fresh Meyer lemon juice (see Tip)

½ teaspoon kosher salt

½ cup (4 oz/125 g) unsalted butter, cut into cubes

1 recipe Meringue Topping (page 96)

½ teaspoon pure vanilla extract

SERVES 8–10

1 Make the gingersnap crust.

2 In a saucepan over medium-high heat, combine the eggs, egg yolks, sugar, cornstarch, lemon juice, and salt. Cook, stirring constantly, until the mixture comes to a boil. Reduce the heat to medium and cook, stirring constantly, until thickened, 6–8 minutes.

3 Pour the mixture through a fine-mesh sieve into a large bowl. Add the butter and stir until melted. Let cool to room temperature. Spread the lemon curd over the crust. Press plastic wrap directly onto the surface and refrigerate for at least 1 hour or up to overnight.

4 Make the meringue. Add the vanilla and beat until the egg whites hold stiff peaks, about 1 minute longer.

5 Preheat the broiler. Place the pie dish on a baking sheet. Pipe or spread the meringue over the lemon curd filling so that it completely covers the pie, leaving no gaps between the crust and the meringue. Broil until the meringue is lightly toasted, about 5 minutes. Refrigerate for at least 2 hours or up to overnight before serving.

 TIP MEYER LEMON JUICE ADDS A SWEET, FLORAL NOTE, BUT REGULAR LEMON JUICE WORKS WELL, TOO. TASTE THE LEMON CURD AND ADD MORE SUGAR, IF NEEDED.

BLACK BOTTOM PIE

This pie is truly a chocolate-lover's dream, with its crunchy chocolate crust and deeply rich chocolate filling. Plenty of toasted meringue peaks and brightly-flavored orange zest complete this masterpiece of a pie.

1 recipe chocolate cookie Wafer Cookie Crust (page 90), baked and cooled

2½ cups (625 ml) whole milk

3 oz (90 g) bittersweet chocolate

4 large egg yolks

¾ cup (6 oz/185 g) sugar

⅓ cup (1 oz/30 g) unsweetened cocoa powder

¼ cup (1 oz/30 g) cornstarch

½ teaspoon kosher salt

2 tablespoons unsalted butter

1 teaspoon pure vanilla extract

1 recipe Meringue Topping (page 96)

½ teaspoon pure vanilla extract

1 tablespoon dark rum

1 teaspoon grated orange zest, for garnish

2 oz (60 g) bittersweet chocolate, chopped or shaved, for garnish

SERVES 8–10

1 Make the wafer cookie crust.

2 In a large saucepan over medium-low heat, combine the milk and chocolate and warm, stirring occasionally, until the chocolate melts.

3 In a large bowl, whisk together the egg yolks, sugar, cocoa powder, cornstarch, and salt. Add the hot milk, ¼ cup (60 ml) at a time, to the egg mixture, whisking constantly, then pour the mixture back into the pan. Stir constantly over medium-high heat until the mixture boils. Reduce the heat to medium and stir constantly until the mixture is thick enough to coat the spoon, 6–8 minutes.

4 Pour the mixture through a fine-mesh sieve into a large bowl. Add the butter and vanilla and stir until the butter is melted. Let cool to room temperature. Pour the filling into the crust. Press plastic wrap directly onto the surface and refrigerate for at least 1 hour or up to overnight.

5 Make the meringue. Add the vanilla and the rum and beat until the egg whites hold stiff peaks, about 1 minute longer.

6 Preheat the broiler. Pipe or spread the meringue over the chocolate filling. Broil until the meringue is lightly toasted, about 5 minutes. Refrigerate for at least 2 hours or up to overnight before serving. Garnish with orange zest and chopped chocolate and serve.

 TIP TO TOAST THE MERINGUE, YOU CAN USE A KITCHEN TORCH INSTEAD OF THE BROILER.

WHITE CHOCOLATE GRASSHOPPER PIE

This light and airy adults-only mousse pie has a subtle hint of mint folded into the creamy and rich white chocolate. Chocolate shavings, which can be made by using a vegetable peeler and a block of dark chocolate, make a pretty garnish.

1 recipe chocolate cookie
Wafer Cookie Crust
(page 90), baked
and cooled

¼ cup (60 ml)
crème de menthe

1 envelope
unflavored gelatin

1½ cups (360 ml)
heavy cream

2 oz (60 g) white chocolate,
chopped

3 large egg yolks

⅓ cup (3 oz/90 g) sugar

1 recipe Whipped Cream
Topping (page 96)

Semisweet chocolate
shavings, for garnish

SERVES 8–10

1 Make the wafer cookie crust.

2 Pour the crème de menthe into a small bowl and sprinkle the gelatin on top. Let stand until the gelatin softens and swells, about 5 minutes.

3 Pour ¾ cup (180 ml) of the cream into the top pan of a double boiler. Place over (not touching) barely simmering water in the bottom pan and warm the cream. Add the white chocolate and whisk until melted. Add the gelatin mixture and whisk until dissolved.

4 In a medium bowl, whisk together the egg yolks and sugar until blended. Add the hot milk, ¼ cup (60 ml) at a time, to the egg mixture, whisking constantly, then pour the mixture back into the double boiler pan. Cook, whisking, until a candy thermometer registers 150°F (65°C), 3–5 minutes. Let cool to room temperature.

5 In the bowl of a stand mixer fitted with the whisk attachment, beat the remaining ¾ cup (180 ml) cream on high speed until soft peaks form, 1–2 minutes. Fold the whipped cream into the white chocolate mixture, then pour the filling into the crust. Refrigerate for at least 2 hours or up to overnight before serving.

6 Top the pie with whipped cream and garnish with chocolate shavings.

 TIP   **FIND CRÈME DE MENTHE AT MOST GROCERIES AND LIQUOR STORES.**

CANDY BAR PIE

This pie is a nut-lover's dream! Use any combination of your favorite nuts here, just make sure they are untoasted and unsalted. The layer of melted chocolate at the bottom of the pie is a welcome surprise.

1 recipe Basic Pie Dough (page 90), rolled into 1 round

6 oz (185 g) semisweet chocolate, melted and cooled slightly

3 cups (15 oz/470 g) assorted raw unsalted nuts, such as pistachios, almonds, peanuts, or walnuts

½ cup (2 oz/60 g) green pumpkin seeds

¼ cup (3 oz/90 g) honey

½ cup (4 oz/125 g) sugar

⅓ cup (80 ml) heavy cream

¼ cup (1¼ oz/40 g) corn syrup

4 tablespoons (2 oz/60 g) unsalted butter, cut into cubes

1 teaspoon pure vanilla extract

Pinch of kosher salt

Flake sea salt, for sprinkling

SERVES 8–10

1 Make the pie dough. Fit the dough round into a 9-inch (23-cm) deep-dish pie dish. Trim the overhang to ½ inch (12 mm), fold the edge under itself, and decoratively flute or crimp. Freeze for 30 minutes.

2 Meanwhile, preheat the oven to 350°F (180°C).

3 Line the crust with aluminum foil and fill with pie weights. Bake until lightly browned and dry to the touch, about 20 minutes. Remove the foil and weights and set on a wire rack to cool completely. Keep the oven set.

4 Spread the melted chocolate over the crust and let cool to room temperature.

5 Spread the nuts and pumpkin seeds on a baking sheet. Toast in the oven until golden brown, about 10 minutes. Let cool. Keep the oven set.

6 In a saucepan over medium heat, combine the honey, sugar, cream, and corn syrup. Stir occasionally until the mixture is slightly thickened and coats the back of the spoon, 2–4 minutes. Remove from the heat. Add the butter, vanilla, and kosher salt and stir until the butter is melted. Stir in the nuts and pumpkin seeds. Pour the filling into the crust. Sprinkle with the flake salt.

7 Bake until the filling is set, about 30 minutes, covering the top with aluminum foil if the nuts brown too quickly. Let cool on a wire rack for at least 4 hours or up to overnight before serving.

 TIP **OTHER TYPES OF NUTS WOULD WORK WELL IN THIS PIE, SUCH AS RAW AND UNSALTED PECANS, CASHEWS, HAZELNUTS, OR MACADAMIA NUTS.**

ORANGECICLE PIE

The well-loved flavor combination of orange and vanilla is a favorite in ice cream treats, so why not replicate it in an amazing pie? This creamy, sweet-tart dessert is sure to become a mainstay of your dessert repertoire.

1 recipe Graham Cracker Crust (page 93), baked and cooled

1 cup (250 ml) whole milk

1 cup (8 oz/250 g) sugar

1 large egg plus 3 large egg yolks

¼ cup (1 oz/30 g) cornstarch

2 tablespoons grated orange zest

¾ cup (180 ml) fresh orange juice

4 tablespoons (2 oz/60 g) unsalted butter, cut into cubes

1 cup (8 oz/250 g) mascarpone cheese

1 recipe Whipped Cream Topping (page 96), for serving

SERVES 8–10

1 Make the graham cracker crust.

2 In a saucepan over medium heat, warm the milk until it just begins to simmer.

3 In a bowl, whisk together the sugar, egg, egg yolks, cornstarch, and orange zest and juice until blended. Add the hot milk, ¼ cup (60 ml) at a time, to the egg mixture, whisking constantly, then pour the mixture back into the pan. Stir constantly over medium heat until the mixture thickens and boils, 3–5 minutes. Remove from the heat, add the butter, and stir until melted. Let cool for 15 minutes, then fold in the mascarpone cheese.

4 Pour the filling into the crust. Refrigerate for at least 2 hours or up to overnight before serving.

5 Serve the pie chilled, topped with whipped cream.

 TIP **FOR A SWEET VARIATION, SWAP OUT THE ORANGE ZEST AND JUICE FOR ANOTHER TYPE OF CITRUS LIKE LIME OR GRAPEFRUIT.**

SWEET-POTATO PIE

This sweet-potato custard pie is a great alternative to pumpkin pie. Make sure you bake it gently, just until the filling is set but still has a slight wobble. The result is a creamy, spiced pie that is perfect with a big dollop of lightly whipped cream.

1 recipe Basic Pie Dough (page 90), rolled into 1 round

1 large egg beaten with 1 teaspoon water

2 cups (18 oz/500 g) peeled, cooked, and mashed sweet potatoes (from about 2½ lb/1.25 kg potatoes)

1 cup (7 oz/220 g) firmly packed light brown sugar

4 tablespoons (2 oz/60 g) unsalted butter, melted and cooled

1 teaspoon cinnamon

½ teaspoon kosher salt

¼ teaspoon ground nutmeg

1 can (12 fl oz/375 ml) evaporated milk

3 large eggs

1 tablespoon pure vanilla extract

SERVES 8–10

1 Make the pie dough. Fit the dough round into a 9-inch (23-cm) pie dish and trim the edges flush with the rim. Tuck the edges under, brush with the egg mixture, and add a braided decoration (see page 14) on the rim. Freeze for 30 minutes.

2 Meanwhile, preheat the oven to 350°F (180°C).

3 Line the crust with aluminum foil and fill with pie weights. Bake until lightly browned, about 20 minutes. Remove the foil and weights and set on a wire rack to cool completely. Keep the oven set.

4 In a blender, blend the sweet potatoes until smooth. Add the brown sugar, melted butter, cinnamon, salt, nutmeg, evaporated milk, eggs, and vanilla and blend until smooth, stopping occasionally to scrape down the sides with a spatula. Pour the filling into the crust.

5 Bake until the center is set and the filling is golden brown, 45–50 minutes, covering the edges with aluminum foil if they brown too quickly. Let cool completely on a wire rack before serving.

 TIP **INSTEAD OF A BRAIDED CRUST, TRY LAYERING SEASONAL CUTOUTS, SUCH AS AUTUMNAL LEAVES OR PUMPKIN DESIGNS, ON THE PIE RIM.**

GRAPEFRUIT CURD PIE WITH BASIL WHIPPED CREAM

Fresh, citrusy grapefruit and fragrant basil shine in this eclectic and delicious pie. For a simpler version, serve with Whipped Cream Topping (page 96) instead, or top each slice with a scoop of vanilla ice cream.

1 recipe Basic Pie Dough (page 90), rolled into 1 round

5 large eggs plus 7 large egg yolks

1½ cups (12 oz/375 g) sugar

⅓ cup (1½ oz/45 g) cornstarch

1 teaspoon grated grapefruit zest

1¼ cups (310 ml) fresh grapefruit juice

¼ cup (60 ml) fresh lemon juice

¼ teaspoon kosher salt

½ cup (4 oz/125 g) unsalted butter, cut into cubes

½ teaspoon freshly ground pepper (optional)

1¼ cups (310 ml) heavy cream

3 tablespoons sugar

½ cup (½ oz/15 g) fresh basil leaves

SERVES 8–10

1 Make the pie dough. Fit the dough round into a 9-inch (23-cm) pie dish. Trim the overhang to ½ inch (12 mm), fold the edge under itself, and decoratively flute or crimp. Pierce the bottom of the crust all over with a fork and freeze for 30 minutes.

2 Meanwhile, preheat the oven to 350°F (180°C). Line the crust with aluminum foil and fill with pie weights. Bake until lightly browned, about 20 minutes. Remove the foil and weights, and cook completely, about 20 minutes longer. Set on a wire rack to cool completely.

3 In a saucepan over medium-high heat, combine the eggs, egg yolks, sugar, cornstarch, grapefruit zest and juice, lemon juice, and salt. Stir constantly until the mixture boils. Reduce the heat to medium and stir constantly until thickened, 6–8 minutes.

4 Pour the mixture through a fine-mesh sieve into a large bowl. Add the butter and pepper (if using) and stir until the butter is melted. Let cool to room temperature. Spread the filling over the crust. Press plastic wrap directly onto the surface and refrigerate for at least 1 hour or up to overnight.

5 Meanwhile, in a small saucepan over medium heat, stir the cream and sugar until the sugar is dissolved and the cream is steaming, about 3 minutes. Remove from the heat. Add the basil leaves. Let steep for 30 minutes. Pour through a fine-mesh sieve. Discard the basil. Chill the cream well, about 2 hours.

6 In the bowl of a stand mixer fitted with the whisk attachment, beat the cream on low speed until stiff peaks form, 3–5 minutes. Raise the speed to medium-high and beat until soft peaks form, about 2 minutes. Pipe or spoon the cream over the pie. Refrigerate for at least 2 hours or up to overnight before serving.

 TIP FOR MORE BASIL FLAVOR IN THE TOPPING, GENTLY CRUSH THE BASIL LEAVES BEFORE STEEPING IN THE CREAM.

BANANA CREAM PIE

The addition of rum and spices takes this special pie over the top. We use vanilla bean for both the flavor and the pretty seeds that show up in the custard, but you can substitute 1 teaspoon pure vanilla extract if you like.

1 recipe vanilla cookie Wafer Cookie Crust (page 90), baked and cooled

4 bananas

6 tablespoons (3 oz/90 g) unsalted butter

¼ cup (2 oz/60 g) firmly packed light brown sugar

½ teaspoon ground allspice

½ teaspoon ground nutmeg

¼ cup (60 ml) rum

3 cups (750 ml) whole milk

⅓ cup (1½ oz/45 g) cornstarch

4 large egg yolks

⅔ cup (5 oz/155 g) granulated sugar

⅛ teaspoon kosher salt

1 vanilla bean, split and seeds scraped, seeds and pod reserved

1 recipe Whipped Cream Topping (page 96)

1 recipe Caramel Sauce (page 45)

SERVES 8–10

1 Make the wafer cookie crust.

2 Halve crosswise 2 of the bananas, then cut into thin slices. In a large sauté pan over medium heat, combine 4 tablespoons (2 oz/60 g) of the butter, the brown sugar, allspice, and nutmeg and stir until the sugar is dissolved, about 2 minutes. Add the banana slices and gently stir until the liquid thickens slightly and the bananas are coated, 3–4 minutes. Remove the pan from the heat, add the rum, then place over medium-high heat, and simmer until the the liquid reduces to a syrup glaze, 4–6 minutes. Let cool to room temperature. Spread the mixture in the crust. Thinly cut the remaining 2 bananas and arrange on top.

3 In a small bowl, whisk together ½ cup (125 ml) of the milk and the cornstarch. In a large bowl, whisk the egg yolks until blended, then slowly whisk in the milk mixture. In a large saucepan over medium heat, combine the remaining 2½ cups (625 ml) milk, the granulated sugar, salt, and vanilla bean seeds and pod and bring to a simmer, stirring to dissolve the sugar. Remove from the heat and let stand for 5 minutes. Discard the vanilla pod.

4 Add the hot milk, ¼ cup (60 ml) at a time, to the egg mixture, whisking constantly, then pour the mixture back into the pan. Stir constantly over medium-high heat until the mixture boils. Reduce the heat to medium and stir constantly until the mixture is thick enough to coat the spoon, 6–8 minutes. Pour through a fine-mesh sieve into a large bowl. Stir in the remaining 2 tablespoons butter until melted. Press plastic wrap directly onto the surface and pierce the plastic a few times with a knife to let the steam escape. Let cool to room temperature. Spread the custard on top of the bananas.

5 Make the topping. Pipe or spoon over the pie. Drizzle the caramel sauce over the cream. Refrigerate for at least 2 hours or up to overnight before serving.

TIP YOU CAN REPLACE THE HOMEMADE CARAMEL SAUCE WITH YOUR FAVORITE JARRED CARAMEL SAUCE FROM THE STORE.

CHOCOLATE-PECAN PIE BARS

With a chocolate crust and plenty of chopped bittersweet chocolate, these bars are the perfect treat for any chocolate and pecan lover. They are also excellent for taking along on a picnic or to a potluck dinner.

1 recipe Chocolate Pie Dough (page 93)

3 large eggs

¾ cup (3¾ oz/115 g) light corn syrup

½ cup (3½ oz/105 g) firmly packed dark brown sugar

½ teaspoon kosher salt

4 tablespoons (2 oz/60 g) unsalted butter, melted and cooled

1 teaspoon pure vanilla extract

2 tablespoons heavy cream

2½ cups (10 oz/315 g) pecans, toasted and chopped

½ lb (250 g) bittersweet chocolate, chopped

Sea salt, for sprinkling

SERVES 10–12

1   Make the pie dough. On a lightly floured work surface, roll out the dough into an 11-by-15-inch (28-by-38-cm) rectangle. Roll the dough around the rolling pin and unroll it into a 9-by-13-inch (23-by-33-cm) baking dish. Gently press the dough into the bottom and sides of the dish. Trim the overhang to ½ inch (12 mm), fold the edge under itself, and decoratively flute or crimp. Freeze for 30 minutes.

2   Meanwhile, preheat the oven to 350°F (180°C).

3   Line the crust with aluminum foil and fill with pie weights. Bake until lightly browned, about 20 minutes. Remove the foil and pie weights and set on a wire rack to cool completely. Keep the oven set.

4   In a large bowl, stir together the eggs, corn syrup, brown sugar, kosher salt, melted butter, vanilla, and cream until smooth and blended. Stir in the pecans and chocolate. Pour the filling into the crust.

5   Bake until the center is slightly puffed and firm to the touch, 30–40 minutes, covering the edges with aluminum foil if they brown too quickly. Let cool on a wire rack until just slightly warm, about 45 minutes, before serving. Sprinkle with sea salt and cut into bars.

 TIP   **INSTEAD OF MAKING THE BARS IN A RECTANGULAR BAKING DISH, FEEL FREE TO USE A 9-INCH (23-CM) PIE DISH.**

MEYER LEMON CHESS PIE

Chess pie, a simple yet flavorful custard pie that is a mainstay of the South, is freshened up with the addition of fragrant Meyer lemons. If you don't have access to Meyer lemons, by all means use more readily available Eureka lemons.

1 recipe Basic Pie Dough (page 90), rolled into 1 round

3 tablespoons all-purpose flour

3 tablespoons finely ground cornmeal

1 cup (8 oz/250 g) sugar

1 teaspoon pure vanilla extract

⅓ cup (2½ oz/75 g) crème fraîche

4 large eggs, lightly beaten

1 cup (250 ml) buttermilk

6 tablespoons (3 oz/90 g) unsalted butter, melted and cooled slightly

Zest of 2 Meyer lemons

SERVES 8–10

1   Make the pie dough. Fit the dough round into a 9-inch (23-cm) deep-dish pie dish. Trim the overhang to ½ inch (12 mm), fold the edge under itself, and decoratively flute or crimp. Freeze for 30 minutes.

2   Meanwhile, preheat the oven to 350°F (180°C).

3   Line the crust with aluminum foil and fill with pie weights. Bake until lightly browned and dry to the touch, about 20 minutes. Remove the foil and weights, and set on a wire rack to cool completely. Keep the oven set.

4   In a large bowl, stir together the flour, cornmeal, sugar, vanilla, crème fraîche, eggs, and buttermilk. Fold in the melted butter and lemon zest. Pour the filling into the crust.

5   Bake until slightly puffed and golden brown, 45–50 minutes, covering the top and edges with aluminum foil if they brown too quickly. Let cool completely on a wire rack before serving.

 TRY FANCYING UP THIS PIE BY TOPPING IT WITH A HANDFUL OF FRESH RASPBERRIES AND A DUSTING OF CONFECTIONERS' SUGAR.

SAVORY PIES

CHICKEN POTPIE WITH MUSHROOMS & THYME

Feed a crowd with this delicious, hefty pie. We love the look and texture of filo dough (which can be found in the freezer section), but you can also use puff pastry or even pie dough for the top. Just bake it until bubbly and the crust is nicely browned.

4 ribs celery

1 lb (500 g) cremini
mushrooms

½ lb (250 g) small potatoes

¾ cup (6 oz/185 g)
plus 2 tablespoons
unsalted butter

1 cup (5 oz/155 g)
plus 2 tablespoons
all-purpose flour

⅓ cup (80 ml) Madeira

2 tablespoons chicken
demi-glace

7 cups (1.75 l) chicken broth

1 large yellow onion, diced

1 tablespoon chopped
fresh thyme

2 teaspoons chopped
fresh tarragon

1 bay leaf

8 cups cubed cooked chicken
(about 3 lb/1.5 kg total)

1 bag (1 lb/500 g) thawed
frozen pearl onions

Kosher salt and freshly
ground pepper

1 recipe Filo Dough Top
(page 95)

1 large egg beaten with
1 teaspoon water

Sea salt, for sprinkling

SERVES 8-10

1 Preheat the oven to 400°F (200°C).

2 Cut the celery into slices ⅛ inch (3 mm) thick. Brush clean and thinly slice the mushrooms. Cut the potatoes into ½-inch (12-mm) dice. In a large 5-qt (5-l) Dutch oven over medium heat, melt the butter. Add the flour and cook, stirring constantly, until the mixture smells fragrant and nutty, about 2 minutes. Whisk in the Madeira and demi-glace. Slowly add the broth, whisking until smooth, and bring to a boil. Add the yellow onion, celery, mushrooms, thyme, tarragon, and bay leaf and cook, stirring occasionally, until the vegetables are almost tender, about 10 minutes. Add the potatoes, chicken, and pearl onions and season with kosher salt and pepper. Cook until the potatoes are tender, about 10 minutes. Let cool for 10 minutes. Discard the bay leaf.

3 Make the filo dough top.

4 Carefully lift the stack of buttered filo and place it on top of the chicken mixture, folding the dough up as necessary along the edges of the pot. Brush the filo with the egg mixture and sprinkle with sea salt.

5 Bake until bubbly and the filo is crisp and browned all over, 15–20 minutes, covering the edges with aluminum foil if they brown too quickly. Let cool for about 10 minutes before serving.

 TIP FOR A DELICIOUS VARIATION, REPLACE THE FILO WITH AN HERBED BISCUIT DOUGH (SEE PAGE 94).

BACON, CHEDDAR & POTATO HOT POCKETS

These savory hand pies are worlds apart from anything you could ever purchase in the store, and they are perfect for tucking into lunch boxes or taking on the road. Choose a good-quality thick-cut bacon for the best flavor.

1 recipe Cream Cheese Dough (page 99)

1 lb (500 g) Yukon gold potatoes, peeled and cut into ½-inch (12-mm) dice

Kosher salt and freshly ground pepper

½ cup (2½ oz/75 g) thawed frozen peas

6 oz (185 g) thick-cut bacon, cooked until crispy and roughly chopped

3 tablespoons unsalted butter

3 tablespoons all-purpose flour

1½ cups (375 ml) whole milk

1 cup (4 oz/125 g) grated Cheddar cheese, plus more for sprinkling

1 teaspoon Dijon mustard

1 large egg beaten with 1 teaspoon water

MAKES 6 HOT POCKETS

1 Make the cream cheese dough. Meanwhile, preheat the oven to 400°F (200°C). Line a baking sheet with parchment paper.

2 On a floured work surface, roll out the dough into a 15-by-16-inch (38-by-40-cm) rectangle about ¼ inch (6 mm) thick. Cut into 12 rectangles, each 4 by 5 inches (10 by 13 cm). Place on the prepared baking sheet and refrigerate until ready to use.

3 Put the potatoes in a saucepan with 1 inch (2.5 cm) of water, cover, and cook over medium heat until the potatoes are tender, about 10 minutes. Drain well, transfer to a large bowl, and toss with 1 teaspoon salt, the peas, and bacon.

4 In a saucepan over medium heat, melt the butter, then add the flour all at once and cook, whisking constantly, until deep golden brown, about 3 minutes. Add ½ cup (125 ml) of the milk and stir until completely incorporated. Repeat with the remaining milk, ½ cup (125 ml) at a time, then stir occasionally until the sauce thickens, about 2 minutes. Stir in the cheese and mustard and season with salt and pepper. Pour the sauce over the potato filling and gently stir to coat. Let cool to lukewarm.

5 On the baking sheet, space 6 of the dough rectangles at least 1 inch (2.5 cm) apart. Brush them with some of the egg mixture, then place about ⅓ cup (1¾ oz/55 g) of the filling in the center of each. Top each with a remaining dough rectangle. Press top and bottom rectangle edges together, then crimp with a fork. Brush the tops with the egg mixture and cut small steam vents in each.

6 Bake until the crusts are golden brown, 18–20 minutes, sprinkle with cheese over the tops during the last 5 minutes of baking, and serve warm.

 TIP IF YOU HAVE DOUGH SCRAPS, GATHER THEM UP AND REROLL TO MAKE MORE HOT POCKETS.

SHEPHERD'S PIE

Here, a hearty filling of ground beef, carrots, peas, and herbs is topped with creamy mounds of buttery mashed potatoes. Drag the tines of a fork across the mash to give it texture, then dot a few small pieces of butter over the top to help it brown up nicely.

2 lb (1 kg) russet potatoes

Kosher salt and freshly ground pepper

2 tablespoons olive oil

2 lb (1 kg) ground beef

1 yellow onion

3 large carrots, peeled and cut into ½-inch (12-mm) pieces

3 ribs celery, cut into ½-inch (12-mm) pieces

2 cloves garlic, minced

⅔ cup (160 ml) white wine

1½ cups (375 ml) chicken or beef broth

2 teaspoons tomato paste

1½ teaspoons Worcestershire sauce

1 teaspoon Dijon mustard

1 tablespoon finely chopped fresh rosemary or thyme

1 cup (5 oz/155 g) frozen peas

4 tablespoons (2 oz/60 g) unsalted butter

1¼ cups (310 ml) half-and-half

½ teaspoon ground nutmeg

½ cup (2 oz/60 g) grated Parmesan cheese

SERVES 6–8

1 Peel and quarter the potatoes. In a saucepan over high heat, bring the potatoes in salted water to a boil. Reduce the heat and simmer until the potatoes are tender, 20–25 minutes. Drain and keep warm.

2 Meanwhile, in a large sauté pan over medium-high heat, warm 1 tablespoon of the oil. Add the beef and season with salt and pepper. Stir occasionally until browned, 7–10 minutes. Transfer to a bowl and discard excess fat from the pan.

3 Meanwhile, finely chop the onion. In the same pan over medium-low heat, warm the remaining 1 tablespoon oil. Add the onion and a pinch of salt and stir occasionally until caramelized, about 10 minutes. Add the carrots, celery, and garlic and stir occasionally until the carrots are just tender, about 5 minutes. Raise the heat to medium-high, add the wine, and simmer until reduced by half, about 5 minutes. Stir in the broth, tomato paste, Worcestershire sauce, mustard, and ½ tablespoon of the rosemary. Stir occasionally until slightly thickened, 6–8 minutes. Add the peas during the last minute of cooking. Return the beef to the pan. Season with salt and pepper. Remove the pan from the heat and cover to keep warm.

4 Meanwhile, place a rack in the upper third of the oven and preheat to 375°F (190°C). Transfer the potatoes to a large bowl and mash with a potato masher. Add the butter and half-and-half and stir until the mixture is well blended. Stir in the nutmeg and season with salt and pepper.

5 Spread the filling evenly in a 9-by-13-inch (23-by-33-cm) or 5-qt (5-l) capacity baking dish. Spread the mashed potatoes evenly on top. Sprinkle with the cheese and the remaining ½ tablespoon rosemary. Bake until the potatoes are lightly browned, 15–20 minutes. Let cool for 5 minutes, then serve warm.

 TIP THIS DISH IS NATURALLY GLUTEN FREE, BUT FOR A THICKER SAUCE, STIR ⅓ CUP (2 OZ/60 G) FLOUR INTO THE FILLING WHEN YOU ADD THE BEEF BACK IN.

QUICHE WITH LEEKS, GOAT CHEESE & FRESH HERBS

We love the versatility of quiche, and this is one of our favorite versions. Filled with buttery leeks, plenty of herbs, and tangy goat cheese, this makes a terrific brunch dish or a light lunch when served with a green salad.

1 recipe Cream Cheese Dough (page 99)

1 tablespoon unsalted butter

1 tablespoon olive oil

3 leeks, white and pale green parts, rinsed and thinly sliced

Kosher salt and freshly ground pepper

4 large eggs

1½ cups (375 ml) whole milk

¼ teaspoon ground nutmeg

1 tablespoon chopped fresh dill

1 tablespoon chopped fresh flat-leaf parsley

½ bunch green onions, white and pale green parts thinly sliced

6 oz (185 g) goat cheese, crumbled

SERVES 8

1 Make the cream cheese dough. On a well-floured work surface, roll out the dough into a 12-inch (30-cm) round and fit into a 9-inch (23-cm) pie dish. Trim the overhang to ½ inch (12 mm), fold the edge under itself, and decoratively flute or crimp. Pierce the bottom of the crust with a fork and freeze for 30 minutes.

2 Meanwhile, preheat the oven to 400°F (200°C).

3 Bake until the edges are lightly browned, about 15 minutes. Let cool briefly on a wire rack. Reduce the oven temperature to 375°F (190°C).

4 In a sauté pan over medium heat, melt the butter with the oil. Add the leeks and ½ teaspoon salt and stir occasionally until the leeks are tender and translucent, about 10 minutes. Let cool slightly.

5 In a large bowl, whisk the eggs until blended. Whisk in the milk, ½ teaspoon salt, ¼ teaspoon pepper, the nutmeg, dill, parsley, and green onions. Stir in the leeks and half of the cheese. Sprinkle the remaining cheese over the crust, then pour in the egg mixture.

6 Bake until the crust is golden brown and the filling is set and slightly puffed, 30–35 minutes, covering the edges with aluminum foil if they brown too quickly. Let cool briefly on a wire rack, then cut the quiche into wedges and serve warm.

 TIP CUSTOMIZE THIS QUICHE AS YOU WISH—SWAP IN YOUR FAVORITE CHEESE OR VEGETABLES, ADD HAM OR COOKED BACON, OR TRY OTHER HERBS AND SPICES.

VEGETABLE POTPIE WITH HERBED BISCUITS

This hearty potpie is chock full of seasonal autumn root vegetables, but feel free to trade in your own favorites depending upon what you have on hand. Sweet potatoes, winter squash, or even broccoli would all be great additions.

3 large carrots

2 Yukon gold potatoes

1 parsnip

1 celery root

1 fennel bulb

2 teaspoons olive oil

1 yellow onion,
finely chopped

Kosher salt and freshly
ground black pepper

1 cup (5 oz/155 g)
thawed frozen peas

6 tablespoons (3 oz/90 g)
unsalted butter

¼ cup (1½ oz/45 g)
all-purpose flour

2 cups (500 ml)
vegetable broth

1½ cups (6 oz/185 g)
grated Gruyère cheese

¼ teaspoon each
ground nutmeg and
cayenne pepper

1 recipe Herbed Biscuit
Dough (page 94)

Flake sea salt, for sprinkling

SERVES 6–8

1   Peel and cut the carrots, potatoes, parsnip, and celery root and cut into ½-inch (12-mm) pieces and put into a large saucepan. Add the fennel and 1 inch (2.5 cm) of water. Cover and cook over medium heat until the vegetables are tender, 10–12 minutes. Drain well.

2   Meanwhile, in a sauté pan over medium heat, warm the oil. Add the onion and a pinch of kosher salt and stir occasionally until lightly caramelized, 6–8 minutes. Transfer to a large bowl. Add the cooked vegetables and toss with a generous pinch of kosher salt. Add the peas and toss to combine. Transfer to a large Dutch oven or a 9-by-13-inch (23-by-33-cm) baking dish.

3   Preheat the oven to 425°F (220°C).

4   In a saucepan over medium heat, melt 4 tablespoons (2 oz/60 g) of the butter, then add the flour all at once and cook, whisking constantly, until deep golden brown, about 3 minutes. Add ½ cup (125 ml) of the broth and stir until completely incorporated. Repeat with the remaining broth, ½ cup (125 ml) at a time, then stir occasionally until the sauce thickens, about 4 minutes. Stir in the cheese, nutmeg, and cayenne and season with kosher salt and black pepper. Pour the sauce over the vegetables and gently stir to coat.

5   Make the herbed dough. Bake until the biscuit top is golden brown and cooked through, 15–20 minutes. Melt the remaining 2 tablespoons butter. Brush the top with the butter and sprinkle with the flake sea salt. Serve warm.

 TIP   SAUTÉED MUSHROOMS MAKE A GREAT ADDITION TO THIS HEARTY VEGETARIAN DISH, WHICH CAN ALSO BE BAKED IN INDIVIDUAL COCOTTES OR RAMEKINS.

TOMATO, CORN & CHEDDAR PIE

When tomatoes, sweet corn, and basil are in season, there's nothing better than this Southern staple. We love the flavor of sharp Cheddar, but shredded mozzarella or Monterey jack would also work nicely.

2 recipes Savory Pie Dough (page 95), rolled into 2 rounds

2½ lb (1.25 kg) heirloom or beefsteak tomatoes, sliced ½ inch (12 mm) thick

Kosher salt and freshly ground pepper

2 tablespoons olive oil

1 yellow onion, diced

2 cloves garlic, minced

1½ cups (6 oz/185 g) grated sharp Cheddar cheese

½ lb (250 g) cream cheese, at room temperature

2 tablespoons whole milk

¼ cup (⅓ oz/10 g) chopped fresh basil

1 cup (6 oz/185 g) fresh or thawed frozen corn

1 large egg beaten with 1 teaspoon water

SERVES 8–10

1 Preheat the oven to 350°F (180°C).

2 Make the pie dough. Fit 1 dough round into a 9-inch (23-cm) deep-dish pie dish and trim the overhang to ½ inch (12 mm). Refrigerate for 30 minutes.

3 Meanwhile, place a wire rack on a baking sheet and arrange the tomato slices on the rack. Sprinkle with salt and roast until soft, 10–15 minutes. Let cool. Keep the oven set.

4 In a sauté pan over medium heat, warm the oil. Add the onion and cook, stirring occasionally, until translucent, 4–5 minutes. Add the garlic and cook, stirring, for 30 seconds. Let cool slightly.

5 In the bowl of a stand mixer fitted with the paddle attachment, beat together the Cheddar cheese, cream cheese, and milk on medium speed until light and creamy, 2–3 minutes. Add the onion mixture, basil, and a large pinch each of salt and pepper and beat until mixed together, about 1 minute.

6 Spread half of the cheese mixture over the crust, then top with the tomatoes in a single layer, slightly overlapping. Sprinkle the corn over the tomatoes and spread the remaining cheese mixture on top. Place the remaining dough round over the filling, trim the edges flush with the rim, and press the top and bottom crusts together. Cut a few steam vents in the top crust. Brush with the egg mixture and sprinkle with salt and pepper.

7 Bake until the crust is golden brown and the filling is bubbling, 40–45 minutes, covering the top and edges with aluminum foil if they brown too quickly. Let cool for about 10 minutes before serving.

 TIP ROASTING THE TOMATOES BEFORE BAKING THEM INSIDE THE PIE PREVENTS THE PIE FROM BECOMING SOGGY.

TAMALE MINI PIES

These spicy little pies, filled with chile-spiked chorizo, beef, tomatoes, black beans, and corn, make a great weeknight meal. Prep the filling up to 2 days ahead, then stir up the corn bread topping at the last minute before baking.

3 tablespoons olive oil

¼ lb (125 g) fresh Mexican chorizo

½ lb (250 g) ground beef

½ yellow onion, diced

1 jalapeño chile, seeded and diced

2 cloves garlic, minced

1 teaspoon ground cumin

1 teaspoon dried oregano

1 teaspoon chili powder

Pinch of red pepper flakes

Kosher salt and freshly ground black pepper

1 can (14 oz/440 g) diced tomatoes with juices

1 cup (250 ml) chicken or beef broth

2 tablespoons tomato paste

1 can (15 oz/470 g) black beans

1½ cups (9 oz/280 g) fresh or thawed frozen corn kernels

1 recipe Corn Bread Topping (page 94)

SERVES 6-8

1 Preheat the oven to 350°F (180°C).

2 In a large sauté pan over medium heat, warm 2 tablespoons of the oil. Add the chorizo and ground beef and stir occasionally until browned and cooked through, 6–8 minutes. Transfer to a bowl. Discard any excess fat from the pan.

3 In the same pan over medium-high heat, warm the remaining 1 tablespoon oil. Add the onion and jalapeño and cook, stirring occasionally, until soft and translucent, 2–3 minutes. Add the garlic and stir for 30 seconds. Add the cumin, oregano, chili powder, red pepper flakes, and a large pinch each of salt and black pepper. Add the tomatoes and their juices, broth, tomato paste, black beans, corn, and the browned meats. Stir well to combine and season with salt and pepper. Divide among 6–8 eight-ounce cocottes or ramekins. Place on a baking sheet.

4 Make the corn bread topping. Spoon the topping on top of the filled cocottes.

5 Bake until the corn bread topping is cooked through and golden brown, about 30 minutes. Serve right away.

 IF YOU DON'T HAVE COCOTTES, TRANSFER THE MIXTURE TO A 9-INCH (23-CM) SQUARE BAKING DISH AND BAKE AS DIRECTED.

BASIC PIE DOUGH

1¼ cups (6½ oz/200 g) all-purpose flour, plus more for dusting

1 tablespoon sugar

¼ teaspoon kosher salt

½ cup (4 oz/125 g) cold unsalted butter, cut into ¼-inch (6-mm) cubes

3 tablespoons very cold water, plus more as needed

MAKES ONE 9-INCH (23-CM) CRUST

1 **To make the dough by hand**, in a large bowl, stir together the flour, sugar, and salt. Using a pastry blender or 2 knives, cut in the butter until the texture resembles coarse cornmeal, with butter pieces no larger than small peas. Add the water and mix with a fork just until the dough comes together.

2 **To make the dough in a food processor**, combine the flour, sugar, and salt in the processor and pulse 2 or 3 times to mix evenly. Add the butter and pulse 8–10 times, until the butter pieces are the size of small peas. Add the water and pulse 10–12 times. Stop the machine and squeeze a piece of dough. If it crumbles, add more of the water, 1 tablespoon at a time, and pulse just until the dough holds together when pinched.

3 Transfer the dough to a work surface and shape into a disk. Refrigerate for 30 minutes.

4 Lightly flour the work surface, then flatten the disk with 6–8 gentle taps of the rolling pin. Lift the dough and give it a quarter turn. Lightly dust the top of the dough or the rolling pin with flour as needed, then roll out into a round at least 12 inches (30 cm) in diameter and about ⅛ inch (3 mm) thick.

WAFER COOKIE CRUST

4½ cups (9 oz/280 g) vanilla or chocolate wafer cookies

1 tablespoon sugar

1 teaspoon kosher salt

½ cup (4 oz/125 g) unsalted butter, melted and cooled

MAKES ONE 9-INCH (23-CM) CRUST

1 Preheat the oven to 350°F (180°C).

2 In a food processor, pulse the cookies until fine crumbs form. Add the sugar and salt and pulse a few times to mix evenly. Add the melted butter and pulse until the texture resembles wet sand. Gently press the mixture evenly into the bottom and up the sides of a 9-inch (23-cm) pie dish, pressing until compact.

3 Bake until the crust is golden brown, about 10 minutes. Let cool completely on a wire rack before filling.

GLUTEN-FREE DOUGH

⅔ cup (3 oz/90 g) almond flour, plus more for dusting

⅓ cup (1 oz/40 g) potato starch

⅓ cup (2 oz/60 g) gluten-free all-purpose flour

1 tablespoon confectioners' sugar

½ teaspoon kosher salt

½ cup (4 oz/125 g) cold unsalted butter, cut into cubes

1 large egg

MAKES ONE 9-INCH (23-CM) CRUST

1 In a food processor, combine the almond flour, potato starch, flour, sugar, and salt and pulse 2 or 3 times to mix evenly. Add the butter and pulse until the texture resembles coarse cornmeal, with butter pieces no larger than small peas. Add the egg and process on low speed until the dough just comes together. Transfer the dough to a work surface and shape into a disk. Wrap well in plastic wrap and refrigerate for at least 1 hour or up to 2 days.

2 When ready to use, substitute this dough into any recipe that uses the Basic Pie Dough to make it gluten-free.

PRETZEL CRUST

4½ cups (6½ oz/200 g) pretzels

1 tablespoon firmly packed light brown sugar

½ cup (4 oz/125 g) unsalted butter, melted and cooled

Pinch of kosher salt

MAKES ONE 9-INCH (23-CM) CRUST

1 Preheat the oven to 350°F (180°C).

2 In a food processor, pulse the pretzels until finely ground. Add the brown sugar, melted butter, and salt and pulse until the texture resembles wet sand. Gently press the mixture evenly into the bottom and up the sides of a 9½-inch (24-cm) pie dish, pressing until compact.

3 Bake until the crust is golden brown, about 10 minutes. Let cool completely on a wire rack before filling.

GRAHAM CRACKER CRUST

14 graham crackers
(about 7½ oz/235 g total)

2 tablespoons firmly packed
light brown sugar

½ cup (4 oz/125 g) plus
2 tablespoons unsalted
butter, melted and cooled

Pinch of kosher salt

**MAKES ONE 9-INCH
(23-CM) CRUST**

1 Preheat the oven to 350°F (180°C).

2 In a food processor, pulse the graham crackers until finely ground. Add the brown sugar, melted butter, and salt and pulse until the texture resembles wet sand. Gently press the mixture evenly into the bottom and up the sides of a 9½-inch (24-cm) pie dish, pressing until compact.

3 Bake until the crust is golden brown, about 10 minutes. Let cool completely on a wire rack before filling.

CHOCOLATE PIE DOUGH

1¼ cups (6½ oz/200 g)
all-purpose flour, plus more
for dusting

1 cup (3 oz/90 g)
unsweetened cocoa powder

1 tablespoon firmly packed
light brown sugar

1 teaspoon espresso powder

¼ teaspoon kosher salt

½ cup (4 oz/125 g) cold
unsalted butter, cut into
¼-inch (6-mm) cubes

3 tablespoons cold coffee,
plus more as needed

**MAKES ONE 9-INCH
(23-CM) CRUST**

1 **To make the dough by hand**, in a large bowl, stir together the flour, cocoa powder, brown sugar, espresso powder, and salt. Using a pastry blender or 2 knives, cut in the butter until the texture resembles coarse cornmeal, with butter pieces no larger than small peas. Add the coffee and mix with a fork just until the dough comes together.

2 **To make the dough in a food processor**, combine the flour, cocoa powder, brown sugar, espresso powder, and salt in the processor and pulse 2 or 3 times to mix evenly. Add the butter and pulse 8–10 times, until the butter pieces are the size of small peas. Add the coffee and pulse 10–12 times. Stop the machine and squeeze a piece of dough. If it crumbles, add more of the coffee, 1 tablespoon at a time, and pulse just until the dough holds together when pinched.

3 Transfer the dough to a work surface and shape into a disk. Refrigerate for 30 minutes.

4 Lightly flour the work surface, then flatten the disk with 6–8 gentle taps of the rolling pin. Lift the dough and give it a quarter turn. Lightly dust the top of the dough or the rolling pin with flour as needed, then roll out into a round at least 12 inches (30 cm) in diameter and about ⅛ inch (3 mm) thick.

CORN BREAD TOPPING

1 cup (5 oz/155 g) cornmeal

1 cup (5 oz/155 g)
all-purpose flour

2 tablespoons sugar

1 tablespoon baking powder

1 teaspoon kosher salt

1 large egg

1 cup (250 ml) buttermilk

4 tablespoons (2 oz/60 g)
unsalted butter, melted
and cooled

**MAKES ENOUGH TO
TOP 6-8 COCOTTES
OR RAMEKINS**

1   In a medium bowl, whisk together the cornmeal, flour, sugar, baking powder, and salt. In a large bowl, whisk together the egg and buttermilk. Add the cornmeal mixture to the egg mixture and stir until just combined. Fold in the melted butter.

2   Scoop the dough on top of the filling to cover.

HERBED BISCUIT DOUGH

1 cup (5 oz/155 g)
all-purpose flour

1 teaspoon salt

1 teaspoon baking powder

½ teaspoon baking soda

4 tablespoons (2 oz/60 g)
cold unsalted butter,
cut into cubes

⅔ cup (160 ml) buttermilk

1 tablespoon chopped fresh
thyme

1 tablespoon chopped fresh
rosemary

**MAKES ENOUGH
TO TOP A 9-BY-13-
INCH (23-BY-33-CM)
BAKING DISH**

1   In a food processor, combine the flour, salt, baking powder, baking soda, and butter and pulse until the texture resembles coarse cornmeal, with butter pieces no larger than small peas. Add the buttermilk, thyme, and rosemary and pulse until combined.

2   Cover the filling with the dough.

SAVORY PIE DOUGH

1¼ cups (6½ oz/200 g) all-purpose flour, plus more for dusting

1 teaspoon sugar

½ teaspoon kosher salt

1 teaspoon freshly cracked pepper

½ cup (4 oz/125 g) cold unsalted butter, cut into ¼-inch (6-mm) cubes

3 tablespoons very cold water, plus more as needed

MAKES ONE 9-INCH (23-CM) CRUST

1 **To make the dough by hand**, in a large bowl, stir together the flour, sugar, salt, and pepper. Using a pastry blender or 2 knives, cut in the butter until the texture resembles coarse cornmeal, with butter pieces no larger than small peas. Add the water and mix with a fork just until the dough comes together.

2 **To make the dough in a food processor**, combine the flour, sugar, salt, and pepper in the processor and pulse 2 or 3 times to mix evenly. Add the butter and pulse 8–10 times, until the butter pieces are the size of small peas. Add the water and pulse 10–12 times. Stop the machine and squeeze a piece of dough. If it crumbles, add more of the water, 1 tablespoon at a time, and pulse just until the dough holds together when pinched.

3 Transfer the dough to a work surface and shape into a disk. Refrigerate for 30 minutes.

4 Lightly flour the work surface, then flatten the disk with 6–8 gentle taps of the rolling pin. Lift the dough and give it a quarter turn. Lightly dust the top of the dough or the rolling pin with flour as needed, then roll out into a round at least 12 inches (30 cm) in diameter and about ⅛ inch (3 mm) thick.

FILO DOUGH TOP

1 box (1 lb/500g) thawed frozen filo dough

½ cup (4 oz/125 g) unsalted butter, melted

MAKES 1 FILO DOUGH TOP

1 Remove the filo sheets from their package and place the stacks of sheets flat on a work surface. Cut the stack crosswise in half; rewrap one half and reserve for another use.

2 Place 1 sheet of filo flat on the work surface; keep the remaining sheets lightly covered with a damp paper towel to prevent drying. Place a second sheet rotated at a slight angle on top of the first and brush lightly with butter. Repeat with the remaining sheets, rotating each one slightly and brushing with butter, to form a rough round that is stacked in the center.

GINGERSNAP CRUST

4 cups (8 oz/500 g)
gingersnap cookies

3 tablespoons sugar

1 teaspoon kosher salt

½ cup (4 oz/125 g) unsalted
butter, melted
and cooled

**MAKES ONE 9-INCH
(23-CM) CRUST**

1 Preheat the oven to 350°F (180°C).

2 In a food processor, pulse the gingersnap cookies until fine crumbs form. Add the sugar and salt and pulse a few times to mix. Add the melted butter and pulse until well combined. Transfer the mixture to a 9-inch (23-cm) pie dish and spread evenly across the bottom and up the sides, pressing until compact.

3 Bake until the crust is set, about 10 minutes. Let cool completely on a wire rack before filling.

MERINGUE TOPPING

5 large egg whites

¼ teaspoon cream
of tartar

½ cup (4 oz/125 g) sugar

**MAKES ENOUGH TO
TOP ONE 9-INCH
(23-CM) PIE**

1 In the bowl of a stand mixer fitted with the whisk attachment, beat together the egg whites and cream of tartar on medium speed until foamy, about 2 minutes. Raise the speed to medium-high and slowly add the sugar. Beat until soft peaks form and the egg whites are shiny and glossy, about 3 minutes. Refer to the specific pie recipe for adding flavorings and beating until the egg whites hold stiff peaks.

WHIPPED CREAM TOPPING

1 cup (250 ml)
heavy cream

½ teaspoon pure
vanilla extract

2 tablespoons
confectioners' sugar

**MAKES ENOUGH TO
TOP ONE 9-INCH
(23-CM) PIE**

1 In the bowl of a stand mixer fitted with the whisk attachment, combine the cream and vanilla. With the mixer on low speed, slowly add the sugar. Raise the speed to medium-high and beat until soft peaks form, about 2 minutes.

OAT CRUMBLE TOPPING

⅓ cup (2 oz/60 g)
all-purpose flour

⅓ cup (1 oz/30 g)
rolled oats

⅓ cup (2½ oz/75 g) firmly
packed light brown sugar

½ teaspoon ground ginger

¼ teaspoon kosher salt

1 teaspoon grated
orange zest

½ cup (4 oz/125 g) unsalted
butter, melted and cooled

**MAKES ENOUGH TO
TOP ONE 9-INCH
(23-CM) PIE**

1 In a medium bowl, whisk together the flour, oats, brown sugar, ginger, salt, and orange zest. Stir in the melted butter. Refrigerate until ready to use.

SHORTBREAD CRUST

6 tablespoons (3 oz/90 g)
unsalted butter, at
room temperature

3 tablespoons
granulated sugar

3 tablespoons firmly packed
light brown sugar

2 large egg yolks

1¼ cups (6½ oz/200 g)
all-purpose flour

1 teaspoon kosher salt

1 teaspoon pure
vanilla extract

**MAKES ONE 9-INCH
(23-CM) CRUST**

1 Preheat the oven to 375°F (190°C).

2 In the bowl of a stand mixer fitted with the paddle attachment, beat together the butter, granulated sugar, and brown sugar on medium speed until light and fluffy, about 3 minutes. Add the egg yolks, flour, salt, and vanilla and beat until just combined, about 2 minutes.

3 Transfer the dough to a 9-inch (23-cm) pie dish and spread evenly across the bottom and up the sides, pressing until compact. Pierce the bottom of the crust all over with a fork and freeze for 20 minutes.

4 Line the crust with aluminum foil and fill with pie weights. Bake until lightly browned, about 20 minutes. Remove the foil and weights. Let cool completely on a wire rack before filling.

ROSEMARY SHORTBREAD CRUST

6 tablespoons (3 oz/90 g) unsalted butter, at room temperature

3 tablespoons granulated sugar

3 tablespoons firmly packed light brown sugar

2 large egg yolks

1¼ cups (6½ oz/200 g) all-purpose flour

1 teaspoon kosher salt

1 teaspoon pure vanilla extract

1 tablespoon finely chopped fresh rosemary

MAKES ONE 9-INCH (23-CM) CRUST

1   Preheat the oven to 375°F (190°C).

2   In the bowl of a stand mixer fitted with the paddle attachment, beat together the butter, granulated sugar, and brown sugar on medium speed until light and fluffy, about 3 minutes. Add the egg yolks, flour, salt, vanilla, and rosemary and beat until just combined, about 2 minutes.

3   Transfer the dough to a 9-inch (23-cm) pie dish and spread evenly across the bottom and up the sides, pressing until compact. Alternatively, refrigerate the dough for 30–60 minutes, then roll out into a 12-inch (30-cm) round, fit into the pie dish and decoratively flute or crimp the edtes. Pierce the bottom of the crust all over with a fork and freeze for 20 minutes.

4   Line the crust with aluminum foil and fill with pie weights. Bake until lightly browned, about 20 minutes. Remove the foil and weights and cook completely, 15–20 minutes longer. Set on a wire rack until cool.

CREAM CHEESE DOUGH

2 cups (10 oz/315 g) all-purpose flour, plus more for dusting

1 teaspoon kosher salt

1 cup (8 oz/250 g) cold unsalted butter, cut into cubes

½ lb (250 g) cream cheese, at room temperature

MAKES ONE 9-INCH (23-CM) CRUST

1   In a food processor, combine the flour, salt, and butter and process until the texture resembles coarse cornmeal, with butter pieces no larger than small peas. Add the cream cheese and pulse a few times, just until the dough comes together. Transfer the dough to a work surface and shape into a disk. Wrap well in plastic wrap and refrigerate for 30 minutes.

INDEX

THE PIE COOKBOOK

Conceived and produced by Weldon Owen, Inc.
In collaboration with Williams-Sonoma, Inc.
3250 Van Ness Avenue, San Francisco, CA 94109

Weldon Owen is a division of Bonnier Publishing.

A WELDON OWEN PRODUCTION

1045 Sansome Street, Suite 100
San Francisco, CA 94111
www.weldonowen.com

Copyright © 2016 Weldon Owen, Inc.
and Williams-Sonoma, Inc.
All rights reserved, including the right of
reproduction in whole or in part in any form.

Printed and bound in China

First printed in 2016
10 9 8 7 6 5 4 3 2

Library of Congress Cataloging-in-Publication
data is available.

ISBN-13: 978-1-68188-157-7
ISBN-10: 1-68188-157-8

WELDON OWEN, INC.

President & Publisher Roger Shaw
SVP, Sales & Marketing Amy Kaneko
Finance & Operations Director Philip Paulick

Associate Publisher Amy Marr
Associate Editor Emma Rudolph

Creative Director Kelly Booth
Associate Art Director Lisa Berman
Senior Production Designer Rachel Lopez Metzger

Production Director Chris Hemesath
Associate Production Director Michelle Duggan

Director of Enterprise Systems Shawn Macey
Imaging Manager Don Hill

Photographer Eva Kolenko
Food Stylist Kim Laidlaw
Prop Stylist Natasha Kolenko

ACKNOWLEDGMENTS

Weldon Owen wishes to thank the following people for their generous support in producing this book:
Kris Balloun, Pranavi Chopra, Gloria Geller, Alexis Mersel, Elizabeth Parson, and Emily Stewart.